macaron
school

macaron
school

Mastering the World's Most Perfect Cookie with 50 Delicious Recipes

camila hurst

Author of *Fantastic Filled Cupcakes*
and Creator of Pies and Tacos

PAGE STREET
PUBLISHING CO.

PAGE STREET
PUBLISHING CO.

First published in 2022 by
Page Street Publishing Co.
27 Congress Street, Suite 105
Salem, MA 01970
www.pagestreetpublishing.com

Distributed by Macmillan, sales in Canada by The Canadian Manda Group.

26 25 24   3 4 5

ISBN-13: 978-1-64567-502-0
ISBN-10: 1-64567-502-5

Library of Congress Control Number: 2021937938

Cover and book design by Laura Benton for Page Street Publishing Co.
Photography by Camila Hurst

Printed and bound in the United States

I dedicate this book to my son,
Luke!

contents

introduction

Welcome to your personal macaron school! This is a book that I've wanted to write for a really long time. I fell in love with macarons a few years ago. In the beginning, I loved their taste, the endless flavor possibilities and the fact that you can decorate them in so many different ways, shapes and colors. Macarons are like a blank canvas. Sharing them on my blog and social media, and connecting with bakers all over the world, has shifted my passion from just making them to also teaching about them in depth as I continue to explore and learn all there is to know about these incredible treats.

The thing about macarons is that they are not like regular cookies and cakes, where you can mostly achieve good results by following a decent recipe step by step. Making macarons is an art of its own. It's like learning how to draw; someone can tell you how to hold the pencil, recommend the best tools and teach you about perspective and proportions, but once you actually start drawing yourself, you will find that it's going to take a lot of practice to get to where you want to be. And most importantly, you will have to figure out your style.

The whole secret to making macarons is just that: finding out what works best for you by equipping yourself with as much knowledge as possible through videos, blogs, books and macaron teachers on Instagram and then, most importantly, putting things into practice and trying them for yourself. When it comes to making macarons, so much can change depending on the weather, the altitude of where you live, the oven you use, the tools you have at your disposal and the brands of ingredients you select—the list goes on and on!

That being said, the challenging aspect of making macarons is what really attracts me and so many others to this craft! It's an art that requires dedication, a great deal of passion, the ability to start over and try again even after one (or ten) epic fails.

I receive dozens of messages, comments and emails every day from bakers all over the world. Some are asking questions, others sharing their success stories and many are just disheartened and frustrated with their macarons. I am here to tell you that it's okay! It takes time! And yes, while some people do have luck from the beginning and start out with amazing macarons, that for sure wasn't the case for me! I completely understand the discouragement around failure, especially because ingredients do cost money and our time is very valuable. I've worked very hard for many years to master (if that's even possible) macarons, and I think all that trial and error has made me an even better teacher, because I've made all the mistakes. So I know what to do, and most importantly, I know what *not* to do. If you have a particular issue with your macarons, I've included plenty of detailed guidance in the Troubleshooting guide on page 153.

The more you inform yourself, and the more knowledge you are able to acquire, the better your chances are at succeeding at making macarons. This book is intended to be a very valuable tool, amongst others, that you should consult to help improve your macaron game—not to mention all of the exciting flavors and amazing filling recipes you will find in these pages! The flavor combo possibilities are infinite, and I am delighted to be sharing some very special and exclusive recipes with you.

Camila Hurst

the basics

There are different methods you can use when making macarons: French, Italian and Swiss. In this book I will focus on the Swiss method.

The French method consists of whipping egg whites with cream of tartar until foamy, and then adding granulated sugar and continuing to whip until the resulting meringue achieves stiff peaks. After that, almond flour and powdered sugar are folded into the meringue to make the batter. While the French method is straightforward and possibly simpler than the Italian and Swiss, it doesn't result in the most stable meringue out of the three methods, which makes it more prone to deflating, breaking or getting overwhipped.

The Italian method is the one with the most steps. It requires heating up a water and sugar syrup to the soft-ball stage while whipping the egg whites to stiff peaks. Then, as soon as the syrup reaches 240°F (116°C), it's whipped in with the egg whites until the meringue cools down and stiff peaks are achieved. A paste of almond flour, powdered sugar and egg whites is folded in to make the batter. This is by far the most high-maintenance method, but it makes a very stable meringue and beautiful shiny shells.

And now we've arrived at the happy medium: the Swiss method—my favorite! It yields a meringue that is more stable than the French method but doesn't involve as many steps or take as much time to make as the Italian, which is why I recommend it for beginners. In the Swiss method—which we will cover in detail in this book—egg whites and sugar get heated over a double boiler just until the sugar melts, then the syrup is whipped to stiff peaks and folded with almond flour and powdered sugar in the process called macaronage.

The reason Swiss meringue is more stable than the French version has to do with the introduction of heat to the process. Dissolving the egg whites and sugar together helps the denaturation process. Denaturation is the unfrilling of the proteins in the egg whites during whipping, which is what forms the stiff peaks and makes the meringue fluffy. Furthermore, the process of melting the sugar increases the viscosity of the syrup that coats the air bubbles in the meringue, contributing to an even stronger meringue structure.

The best way to master macarons is to understand the three main stages of making the batter: the meringue stage, the macaronage and the oven. Once you understand exactly what the meringue is supposed to look like, the perfect stage of the macaronage and how to best use your oven, things will become much easier.

first, let's discuss the meringue: The meringue should be whipped to stiff peaks. The peaks should be shooting straight up, not bending down to the side. To identify this stage, keep an eye on the meringue as it whips. If the meringue starts to become fluffy around the whisk, you can start checking your peaks. You'll know you are getting close to this stage when the meringue is balling up around the whisk and looks glossy.

Dip the whisk in the bowl with the meringue and swirl it around to grab a good amount of meringue, then hold it upright. You only need a peak that measures 2 to 3 inches (5 to 8 cm); if the peak is any longer than that, it will probably bend down, giving you the impression that the meringue isn't whipped enough.

If the peak is shooting up without bending to the side, and if the meringue around the base of the whisk has a nice soft and fluffy cloud-like formation, it is probably done.

If the meringue is under whipped, the peaks will be long and seem very elastic. The meringue also won't be balling up around the whisk, but it will seem thin and soft, so continue to whip for another few minutes.

Perfectly whipped meringue

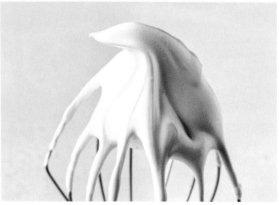

Underwhipped meringue

Overwhipped meringue

If the meringue is overwhipped, the peaks will be very short, pointing straight up and will seem chunky—you will feel a lot of resistance as you try to swirl the whisk around in the bowl to grab the meringue to test it. Depending on how much the meringue has been overwhipped, it may not be worth it to proceed with the recipe. However, in most cases, overwhipped meringue will cause issues that can often be overlooked, such as frilly feet, hollow shells or a porous shell surface, and macarons with these issues can still be enjoyed. This is also a part of the learning process, so I don't recommend tossing an overwhipped meringue unless it is really chunky.

If you are still unsure about finding the sweet spot for meringue, it can be helpful to stop the mixer every 30 seconds to check once it gets to the final stages of whipping—this way the meringue won't have a chance to become over whipped.

To get a better understanding of how to identify issues that could result from overwhipping or underwhipping the meringue, I recommend checking out the Troubleshooting guide on page 153.

Once you have the perfect meringue, it's time to master the macaronage.

macaronage is the act of folding the dry ingredients—almond flour and powdered sugar—with the meringue.

Perform the macaronage by folding the batter in a J motion with the spatula, cutting through the middle and going down and around the batter. Once the batter is incorporated, use the spatula to spread it around the sides of the bowl, squishing the air bubbles out as you press down on the batter with the spatula.

You should stop folding once the batter is flowing off the spatula slowly and effortlessly, almost like lava. You should be able to draw several figure eights with the batter that is flowing off the spatula, and even after the batter breaks up, it should still continue to flow slowly. The batter that falls back into the bowl should take 10 to 15 seconds to start incorporating with the batter that's already there.

When you pipe the batter, it should spread out gently and the top should smooth out, without having a pointy tip on the surface. If the batter spreads out too much and becomes misshapen, it's probably overmixed, and if it does have a pointy tip on the top, it's undermixed.

Other signs that indicate undermixed batter include if the batter is falling off the spatula in chunks instead of flowing in a slow stream, or if the batter flowing off the spatula is taking too long to incorporate with the batter that's already in the bowl.

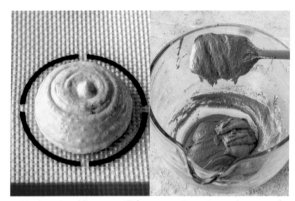

Undermixed batter will form a pointy tip at the top of the shells and will fall off the spatula in chunks.

If the batter is overmixed, it will fall continuously, without stopping, and it will seem very runny. If the batter has a ribbon-like consistency, it's probably overmixed. A perfectly mixed batter should fall slowly rather than quickly.

Take a look at the Troubleshooting guide on page 153 to learn about the possible outcomes for overmixed or undermixed batter—this can help you identify future issues with the macaronage and recognize when you need to stir less or more.

lastly, you should study your oven. First, make sure to use an oven thermometer. Second, figure out the best temperature for your oven. Each oven is very different. Some people bake my recipe at a lower temperature because 325°F (160°C) is too hot for their oven. To figure out the best temperature

Overmixed batter will lose a defined shape once piped.

for your oven, try piping one batch of macarons between four different trays, then bake each tray at a different temperature or oven rack level, write down the results and compare. Experiment as much as necessary until you find the sweet spot.

Oven temperature can have a huge effect on the success of your macarons. Just a few degrees higher or lower can make all the difference in the results. For more details on some of the issues that can come up if your oven is too hot or too cold (and how to solve them!), see the Troubleshooting guide on page 153.

When it comes to macarons, it's all about experimenting and finding out what works best for you. Join macaron Facebook groups, watch YouTube videos and follow different teachers on Instagram. At the beginning of my journey, I kept a notebook with me and always wrote down my experiments and results, which helped me narrow down what I could be doing wrong and kept my research meaningful.

ingredients

The four basic ingredients you need to make macarons are egg whites, granulated sugar, powdered sugar and almond flour. I also like to add egg white powder to my shells, but depending on the humidity (or lack thereof) of the baking environment, this can have an impact on the final results, which I'll cover in more detail on page 15. Here we will cover each ingredient individually.

egg whites

I prefer fresh egg whites instead of old ones. They form a stronger meringue because the proteins are tighter than those of older egg whites. When making macarons, if you happen to have multiple cartons of eggs in your fridge, always use the newer eggs for their egg whites.

A lot of people talk about "aging" the egg whites, which means cracking the eggs and separating the whites, then covering the whites with a piece of plastic wrap and letting them sit for a few days in the fridge, or even at room temperature, to let some of the water content of the whites evaporate. I have experimented with aged egg whites and with freshly cracked whites many times and don't find using aged egg whites to have any impactful changes in the meringue.

Another question I get a lot is about the temperature of the egg whites—specifically if they have to be at room temperature. If I don't have any room-temperature egg whites to make macarons, I simply use cold ones. It won't make a difference in the Swiss meringue since the egg whites will be heated with the sugar and turned into a syrup before being whipped. The only difference is that it may take a bit longer for the sugar to completely melt over the double boiler if cold egg whites are used.

You can also use carton egg whites, though they will take a bit longer to whip and the meringue made from carton egg whites is naturally softer than the meringue made from fresh whites, which means it may be harder to pinpoint when to stop whipping it. If using carton egg whites, I strongly recommend adding cream of tartar, egg white powder or even both to the meringue. I discuss both of those ingredients further on page 15.

I do not recommend using coconut sugar or any other sugar substitutes such as stevia or erythritol, because it simply won't work. As explained previously, the sugar is essential to the structure of the meringue, and coconut sugar and other sugar substitutes are unable to keep this structure intact.

You can, however, use brown sugar or even cane sugar, as long as the crystals aren't too large. Cane sugar will not affect the flavor of the macarons, while brown sugar will give the shells a deeper and slightly nutty flavor, as well as a naturally tan color.

powdered sugar

Powdered sugar and confectioners' sugar are the same thing. In the United States, most brands have cornstarch (or tapioca flour) added to the sugar. However, a lot of bakers all over the world use pure powdered sugar without issue. If you would like to add cornstarch to the powdered sugar, I recommend adding about 5 grams along with the powdered sugar when sifting the dry ingredients.

Powdered sugar is responsible for the remarkable feet in macarons. Recipes with a lower ratio of powdered sugar will generally produce smaller feet. Its main role is not only to provide sweetness but also to help soak up the moisture from the batter, which contributes to the formation of beautiful feet.

almond flour

It's very important to find a brand of almond flour that is finely ground and dry. Some brands are way too coarse or oily, and you may have to experiment with different brands to find the perfect almond flour. My favorite brand of almond flour is Blue Diamond®, and I've been using it exclusively for quite some time now.

Personally, I don't like making my own almond flour from whole almonds. It takes a professional-grade food processor to be able to finely grind the almond flour without releasing any oils. The minute oils begin to be released, the batter will be severely impacted by it, leaving you with wrinkled or porous macarons, since oils destroy the protein bonds that keep the air bubbles in place to form the structure of the meringue.

granulated sugar

White granulated sugar is added to the meringue when making macarons, and with the Swiss method, the granulated sugar is mixed with the egg whites over a double boiler to form a syrup before whipping the meringue.

Adding sugar to the meringue will stabilize it because the sugar dissolves in the water particles, creating a stronger barrier to protect the air bubbles.

A lot of people like to use caster sugar, or superfine sugar, when making meringue—especially if using the French method, which involves adding the sugar directly to the whipping egg whites. For French macarons, using caster sugar will help the sugar melt faster and dissolve better with the egg whites in order to form the meringue. When it comes to the Swiss method, you are fine using regular white granulated sugar, since the sugar gets melted before the whipping starts.

You can always sift the sugar to eliminate any larger crystals before starting, but if you do that, be sure to weigh the sugar after sifting it to ensure you still have the correct amount.

Additionally, I don't recommend processing the almond flour in the food processor before making the macarons in an attempt to make it finer, since this action can also release oils.

My recommendation is to find a brand of almond flour that is already finely ground and does not need to be processed.

You can tell the quality of the almond flour by touching it. If it feels wet or oily, it's not great. You can also try sifting it, and if there's a lot of almond flour leftover in the sifter that didn't pass through, it means the flour is too coarse, and you'll need to find a different brand.

You can store the almond flour in an airtight container in the fridge, freezer or at room temperature. It is important to let the almond flour come to room temperature if it's stored in the fridge or freezer, and always check to see if the flour has become moist during storage.

A helpful trick to remedy moist or lightly oily almond flour is to spread it on a baking sheet and bake it in an oven preheated to 200°F (93°C) for 30 minutes, stirring halfway through, to dry the almond flour. Remove the baking sheet from the oven and let it cool down completely before using the flour. I say "lightly oily" almond flour, because it's normal for some batches to be a bit oilier than others. However, if the flour is too greasy, I recommend not using it for macarons at all.

And finally, always use fresh flour. If your almond flour has been sitting in the pantry or fridge for a couple of months, I would buy a fresh bag to make macarons.

egg white powder

Egg white powder is an optional ingredient that you don't necessarily need to make macarons, but it can improve the quality of the meringue, and therefore the quality of the final macaron shells.

Egg white powder is not the same as meringue powder, even though some people use meringue powder in the same way. Egg white powder consists of just dried egg whites, while meringue powder also has cornstarch, sugar and other additives included in the formula.

The way egg white powder works is by adding more protein to the meringue without adding any extra water content, which makes it act like a stabilizer that helps form a strong meringue.

However, when the weather is really dry, I skip the egg white powder. I keep a hygrometer (humidity thermometer) in my kitchen, and if it indicates that the humidity is anywhere below 20 percent, I leave the egg white powder out. The weather and humidity have a huge impact on the meringue; if the weather is super humid, the meringue will absorb water particles from the air, and if the weather is super dry, it will also dry out the meringue. Whenever I make macarons with added egg white powder on a dry day, the shells will immediately dry as I pipe them, not even leaving me enough time to poke the air bubbles without leaving streaks on the shells.

If you live in a humid place, egg white powder can be an extremely beneficial ingredient to experiment with.

As a rule of thumb, I go for 4 grams of egg white powder per 100 grams of plain batter. For chocolate, matcha or shells with freeze-dried fruit powder, I decrease the amount of egg white powder to 2 grams, since the added flavoring powders will also make the batter dryer.

I recommend experimenting with egg white powder, and if it makes your batter too dry, either try whipping the meringue less or adding a bit less powder next time, and always make sure to check the humidity levels of your kitchen.

cream of tartar

You don't typically see cream of tartar being added to Swiss meringue recipes. That being said, I have experimented with adding cream of tartar several times to my macarons, and it works great! I prefer adding egg white powder, and I don't usually add both together unless I'm using carton egg whites. But during those dry winter days, I've added cream of tartar to my meringue, and it has helped make it strong and beautiful.

The acidity of cream of tartar helps the egg whites achieve their full volume potential. Cream of tartar makes the meringue stable by helping hold the water and air particles in place. Its acidity also helps lower the pH of the egg whites, changing the electrical charge of the proteins, making them more sensitive to the denaturation process (unfrilling of the proteins) and increasing the hydrogen ions present in the meringue, which prevents the molecules from bonding too tightly in the case of overwhipping.

I add ¼ teaspoon of cream of tartar per 100 grams of egg whites when using. Add the cream of tartar directly to the syrup once you begin whipping it.

cocoa powder

When making chocolate shells, my recipe calls for 14 grams of cocoa powder. This is a high amount compared to many other recipes out there.

If your shells are coming out wrinkly or porous, here are a few things to observe.

First, check how fresh the cocoa powder is. A fresh batch will work best, as older cocoa powder may begin to release oils.

Second, be sure to use a brand of cocoa powder (or cacao powder) with a low amount of fat. You are looking for a cocoa powder that has no more than 0.5 grams of fat per tablespoon. Too much fat will affect the meringue, destroying some of the protein bonds that keep the air and water particles in place, which will result in porous or wrinkly shells. I don't recommend using Dutch-process cocoa powder, as it contains a lot more fat than regular cocoa powder. For this same reason, be careful of brands that are a mixture of Dutch-process and regular cocoa powder, such as Hershey's Special Dark.

Third, try decreasing the amount of cocoa powder to 5 to 10 grams instead of 14 grams, and add extra brown food coloring for a deeper chocolate color.

food coloring

The best kind of food coloring to add to macaron batter is gel- or powder-based. Don't add water-based food coloring to the batter, because it is very diluted and you would need a lot of it to achieve a nice color. Besides that, even if you add a little bit, the water in it will add extra moisture to the shells and might dissolve the protein bonds holding the meringue structure in place.

Gel-based food coloring is my go-to; it's highly concentrated and it gets incorporated quickly with the batter, which gives you a better chance to control the final color. To obtain a vibrant color, you will need to add a lot of food coloring to the batter, so if your shells are coming out faded or browned, it's simply because you aren't using enough food coloring. The only issue with adding too much food coloring is that it will affect other aspects such as macaronage, resting and baking time. The batter will probably require less folding, since it will have more liquid in it, the resting time might be much longer and the baking time might be longer as well. If you are a beginner, I recommend sticking to just a few drops of food coloring, and as you gain more confidence and are able to identify the consistency of the batter more easily, and adjust to the "wetter" batter, you can begin experimenting with bolder and more vibrant tones.

Powder-based food coloring is also a great option—it is even more concentrated than gel food coloring and doesn't add any extra moisture to the batter. If using powder-based food coloring, add it along with the meringue at the final stages of whipping, since it can take a while for the color to fully develop. And if using gel-based food coloring, add it along with the dry ingredients.

materials needed

The quality of your tools is very important when making macarons—having great tools will make your life much easier. You may have to shop around and try different brands until you find your favorite ones, but investing in durable tools that will be reliable and help ensure the best results is always worth it. Also keep in mind that some tools may need regular replacement, such as baking sheets, silicone mats and oven thermometers. The following tools I discuss are indispensable in my macaron making.

scale

Having a digital food scale is essential when making macarons. Each time you scoop a cup of almond flour, you won't always obtain the exact same amount. One egg white could be anywhere from 30 to 40 grams, and that can make a huge difference. There are a lot of variables when making macarons, such as the weather, the oven, the humidity levels and the consistency of the meringue and batter, so the things that we *can* control, we absolutely *must*! The weight of the ingredients is one of those things. Be sure to accurately weigh all of your ingredients with a scale. A kitchen scale is inexpensive and may even save you money since it will help you waste fewer ingredients.

While many of the recipes in this book include ingredient measurements in metrics and US conversions, I strongly suggest you use just the metric measurements for the greatest chance for success. In fact, you will even notice that for the shells recipes in Chapter 2 (page 22), I do not provide US measurements at all, as it is essential that you use a digital scale to measure your ingredients for these recipes.

oven thermometer

Probably the most valuable tool when making macarons is an oven thermometer. I have three in my oven—two of them hanging in the front of the oven on opposite sides and one in the middle center of the oven.

Built-in oven thermometers are not accurate at all. They are usually placed somewhere in the back of the oven or along the walls, where they're subject to drafts and temperature fluctuations. Built-in oven thermometers hardly ever tell the exact temperature from the middle of the oven, where the cookies are actually being baked. Not to mention that ovens cycle in order to maintain an average temperature around what you set it to, so ovens switch the heating element on and off in order to keep a somewhat constant temperature. As a result, the temperature you set your oven to is hardly ever the actual temperature at which you're baking your food.

You need an oven thermometer to monitor the temperature and either turn it up or down according to what's going on inside the oven. For example, with my current oven, I have to set the temperature to 300°F or 305°F (150°C) in order to have it at 325°F (160°C), which is the best temperature for baking macarons with my oven.

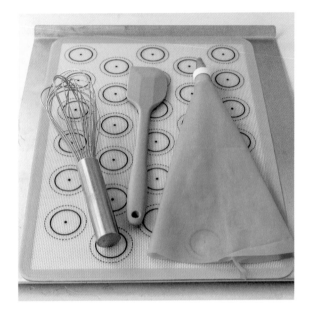

macaron mats

I like to use macaron mats—silicone baking mats with round piping templates printed on them. They help ensure each macaron has a smooth bottom and a consistently round shape. I find that parchment paper wrinkles, giving the macarons wrinkly, uneven bottoms. Some people love baking with Teflon™ sheets, but please note that Teflon sheets will require a lower baking temperature because Teflon is such a good heat conductor.

Replace your mats as needed if they begin accumulating residues or getting sticky and hard to clean. Sometimes a good soak in vinegar and warm soapy water can do the trick, but after a year or so, you might want to replace your mats with new ones.

piping bags

You will need piping bags to pipe the macaron batter. I like to use reusable silicone piping bags so I don't have to waste so much plastic. Always remember to designate specific bags for macaron batter and for frosting, because the frosting will leave traces of grease and butter, and oils do not work well with macaron batter. Fat particles can destroy your meringue by popping the air bubbles in it.

piping tips

To pipe the macaron batter, I like to use a round piping tip that is either ¼ or ½ inch (6 mm or 1.3 cm) in diameter. If piping detailed shapes, I'll use smaller tips, but for the regular circular macaron shape, these are my favorite tip sizes. If you use the same piping tips for buttercream and macaron batter, I recommend soaking them in vinegar and warm soapy water for a while to eliminate any grease residues. Using a tube cleaning brush to scrub the insides of the piping tips is even better.

baking trays

You will need a few baking trays, or at least two, if making just one batch of macarons. I prefer aluminum trays with short rims—less than 1 inch (2.5 cm) tall—or no rims at all. Rimless baking sheets are great, and I've been using them a lot. Stay away from trays with tall rims, trays made of steel or trays that are dark in color.

Tall rims prevent the air and the heat from circulating properly, which can cause lopsided or even cracked macarons. If you only have trays with tall rims on hand, you can always flip the trays upside down and bake your macarons on the underside of the trays.

Aluminum conducts heat better than steel, so using aluminum trays ensures the heat is more evenly distributed while the macarons are baking. Aluminum also cools down faster, so the macarons won't continue to bake for too long after they come out of the oven.

Using dark trays can cause the macarons to crack and the feet to spread out too much because dark trays retain more heat than light colored ones. They can also result in overbaked macarons that turn out crunchy, or hollow macarons that bake faster on the outside than in the middle.

Also make sure the trays you are using aren't warped. The baking trays must be flat and straight. If the trays get warped, be sure to replace them, as warped trays will cause uneven heat distribution or misshapen macarons.

mixer

You will need an electric mixer to make macarons. Macarons can require up to 30 minutes of mixing time, depending on the speed setting and size of the batch, so using a stand mixer is the most convenient option. Hand mixers will also work—I have used them many times to make macarons. When making smaller batches of macarons, it is actually better to use a hand mixer, because oftentimes, the whisk of the stand mixer won't reach the bottom of the bowl and won't be able to whip a small amount of egg whites properly. So, if you are halving a recipe and making a smaller batch, use a hand mixer instead of a stand mixer, or make sure the whisk of your stand mixer reaches the bottom of the bowl.

sifter

A sifter is very necessary to make macarons. Look for a fine-mesh sieve; I like those with a double mesh that retain the larger pieces of almond flour.

bowls

You will also need bowls to sift the ingredients into, to place on top of the double boiler to melt the sugar and egg whites in and to separate the batter to make different colors. I recommend heavy-duty glass bowls. Stay away from plastic bowls. They are not heat-proof, so they can't be placed over a hot pan to form the double boiler, and the plastic can harbor traces of fat and grease, which will ruin your meringue.

spatulas

It's good to find a few reliable, sturdy silicone spatulas for your tool kit. I like to keep my macaron batter spatulas separate from all the other ones so I don't accidentally use them for meringue. This way, there's no chance they will have grease particles from buttercream or other baked goods on them. You may need several spatulas, especially if you are making different colors of meringue, so invest in a few dependable ones. If you notice your spatulas have tears in them, throw them out and replace them, because those tears can accumulate food and other particles inside.

whisk

You will need at least one whisk to be able to mix the sugar and egg whites over the double boiler before whipping. I like to have an exclusive one just for macarons that doesn't get used for other recipes like butter-based sauces and such, so there aren't any surprise grease particles to worry about.

storage containers

I like to refrigerate and freeze macarons in heavy-weight, airtight plastic containers.

before you start

Here are all the preparation steps you need to take before you start making macarons. Being organized will pay off, so it's important to take your time and make sure everything is set up right to ensure a smooth ride while making the batter.

The very first step is to preheat your oven. My current oven is electric, and not only does it take a while to preheat, but the longer it preheats, the more stable the temperature in the oven will be throughout the baking process. If your oven suffers from a lot of temperature fluctuation, try preheating it for longer, as this will help stabilize the oscillation.

Next, make sure you have gathered all the ingredients and tools you will need. Each recipe in this book features a comprehensive list of ingredients and tools necessary to successfully make it.

Set aside the baking trays and macaron mats. To make one batch using the recipes in this book you will need two baking trays and two macaron mats or two pieces of parchment paper.

Line the baking trays with the mats or parchment paper and set them aside.

Set aside a bowl for the egg whites and sugar, and pour water in a small saucepan up to 2 inches (5 cm) high to form the double boiler. Grab a whisk to be able to mix the whites and sugar.

Get your mixer ready with the whisk attachment.

Set aside some spatulas, whatever food coloring you will use, and as many bowls as needed if you plan on making different colored batters from the same batch of macarons.

Wipe everything down with vinegar. Dip a paper towel in vinegar, and then wipe down your baking trays and macaron mats, the whisks, spatulas, bowls and everything else that will touch the macaron batter. The vinegar helps get rid of any grease particles that may be on the tools and materials. Grease can weaken the protein bonds that form the meringue, making it unstable or even broken, so you'll want to take care of it before beginning to make your macarons.

Set aside as many piping bags as you will need and line them with your piping tip of choice. I like to use a small or medium round piping tip that's ¼ or ½ inch (6 mm or 1.3 cm) in diameter. Then place the piping bag inside of a cup, with the tip on the bottom, and flip the top of the bag around the edges of the cup; this will help you transfer the batter to the piping bag effortlessly.

Set aside some bag ties to secure the top of each bag closed after transferring the batter. The bag ties will help the batter not dry out or escape through the top as you are piping, and it will give you more control of the piping process since you'll be able to focus on the dominant hand that is applying pressure to release the batter.

Weigh all the ingredients: the egg whites, egg white powder (if using), granulated sugar, powdered sugar, almond flour and any other ingredients you might be adding such as cocoa powder, matcha, etc.

Sift the dry ingredients together and set them aside.

Having all of the ingredients and materials you will use set aside before starting will make a huge difference and help make the process smoother.

tips and tricks for mastering macarons

Here I have gathered some of the most helpful tips that can really improve your macaron game! They are based on frequently asked questions that I get daily.

- Always have an oven thermometer. As discussed on page 17, built-in thermometers are not accurate at telling the precise temperature that is inside the oven, and when making macarons, even just a difference of five degrees can change everything. For example, I bake my macarons at 325°F (160°C), however, I have to set my oven to 305°F (150°C), because if I actually set it to 325°F (160°C), the temperature will shoot all the way up to 350°F (175°C).

- If using a convection oven, lower the temperature indicated in recipes by at least 10 percent.

- To keep white- or pastel-colored macarons from browning, cover them with foil during the final 5 minutes of baking.

- To make brighter macarons, simply use more food coloring, but be careful not to overmix the batter as you continue to stir in more color. The earlier you add the food coloring during the macaronage process, the better.

- Keep in mind that the color of your macarons will fade as the shells bake, so always make the batter a tone more vibrant than what you'd like the final result to be.

- Whip the meringue at a lower speed (speed 4 or 6 on a KitchenAid® stand mixer). This may take longer, but it often produces a stronger, more stable meringue.

- If your macarons are too crunchy, place a slice of bread or a brown sugar saver inside your storage container with the filled macarons. Use a piece of plastic wrap or parchment paper to avoid direct contact between the macarons and the bread or sugar saver. Refrigerate the container overnight, and on the next day, the macarons should have softened up as they absorbed the moisture from the bread or brown sugar saver.

- Macaron shells can be frozen for up to a couple of months. To fill them after freezing, simply remove them from the freezer and pipe the filling in the center—there is no need to thaw them before doing so. Filled macarons can usually be frozen for up to a month, or even longer. If the macaron features a wet filling, such as jam or curd, you can brush a bit of melted chocolate on the bottom of the macarons and let it dry before filling them. The melted chocolate will act as a barrier to protect the macaron shells from getting too soggy. This is not a guarantee that they won't get soggy, but it can help.

- It's not recommended to reduce the amount of sugar in the shells. The sugar is very important for the structure of the macarons. If you are looking for macarons that are less sweet, use fillings such as dark chocolate ganache, tart jam or French buttercream. Some of these fillings for less sweet macarons can be found in the following recipes: Peppermint Mocha Macarons (page 70), Pomegranate Dark Chocolate Macarons (page 108), Apricot Macarons (page 94) and Cassis Macarons (page 117).

- You can substitute the almond flour for all-purpose flour. It might take a couple of tries to get the consistency of the batter right because it will feel a bit stiffer and can be harder to tell when to stop stirring. Also, the taste of the all-purpose flour shell will be a bit chalky on its own, but once filled, a lot of people won't be able to tell the difference.

- Always let the macarons mature overnight, or even up to 2 days, before serving. Maturing will develop the flavors in the macarons and soften up the shells.

- Using a rimless baking sheet can help prevent lopsided or cracked macarons—issues caused by tall rims that hamper even heat distribution.

- If you live in a humid climate, try experimenting with adding egg white powder to the shells, and also with any no-rest methods. If the shells rest in a humid environment, they will end up absorbing humidity from the air.

shells

And now, it's time for the recipes to begin! We will start with ten different shell flavors, so that you can pair them with the fillings in the later chapters. The first recipe will be for Plain Macaron Shells (page 24), and you should read it thoroughly, as it contains all the details and elaborate explanations about how to make macaron shells. Then, in the next few pages, I will show the flavor variations and how to incorporate them into the macaron shells, with a more brief explanation of the process. Are you ready to start your macaron journey?

plain macaron shells

This recipe for plain shells is the one I use for most of my flavors and should be the first one you try if you are a macaron beginner. It's easier to start with a plain recipe because there are fewer variables that can interfere with the final result. Mastering the basics is always a good idea before attempting to add flavorings to the shells.

When I began making macarons, I used to focus solely on flavoring the filling and leaving the shells plain. While I continue to believe that the filling is the star of the show, over the years I have begun flavoring the shells of my macarons with nuts and powders. Still, it is essential to have a reliable plain shell recipe as a go-to.

yield: 40 (1½" [4-cm]) macaron shells

105 g almond flour
105 g powdered sugar, sifted
100 g granulated sugar
4 g egg white powder (optional)
100 g egg whites
Gel-based food coloring of choice (optional)

Sift the almond flour and powdered sugar together.

Preheat the oven to 325°F (160°C). Sift the almond flour and powdered sugar into a bowl and set it aside.

Bring a pot of water to a low simmer over medium heat and place a heat-proof bowl on top. You can also use a double boiler if you prefer. The water shouldn't touch the bottom of the bowl.

Melt the sugar and egg whites over a double boiler.

Start whipping on low and gradually increase the speed.

Pour the granulated sugar and egg white powder (if using) into the heat-proof bowl and whisk over the simmering water. It's important to whisk the egg white powder and sugar together before adding the egg whites to prevent any clumps from forming.

Add the egg whites to the bowl and whisk the ingredients together for 2 to 4 minutes, until the sugar has completely melted. The syrup should not get hot—it should stay lukewarm (around 120°F [48°C]) and should not feel hot to the touch—as heat will tighten the protein bonds in the egg whites and cause wrinkled macarons or other meringue issues. Keep the mixture on top of the simmering water just until the sugar melts. Test the doneness of the syrup by touching it and rubbing it between your fingers. When you don't feel any sugar granules, remove the bowl from the heat.

Wipe down the bottom of the bowl with a towel so that the water from the condensation doesn't drip into the meringue, then transfer the syrup to the bowl of a mixer.

Continue to whip until stiff peaks are achieved.

Begin by whipping on low speed for 30 seconds. Increase the speed to medium-low for another 30 seconds, and then increase it to medium. Finish whipping on medium or medium-high until the meringue achieves stiff peaks. The total whipping time will depend on your mixer and the speed you are using, but it should be 10 to 30 minutes. I whip my meringue on speed 6 of my KitchenAid, and it takes me about 10 minutes. When the meringue starts to get fluffy and the whisk starts leaving streak marks on the meringue, start checking the meringue for stiff peaks.

(continued)

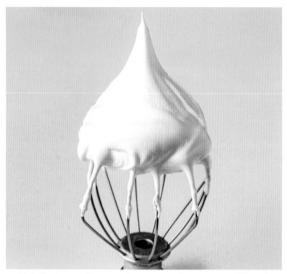

This is the perfect meringue consistency: a stiff peak shooting straight up.

Add the sifted dry ingredients to the meringue.

To check the meringue, stop the mixer, dip the whisk in the meringue and pull it up. When you hold the whisk upright, the peaks should be shooting straight up, not bent down to the side. If the peaks are too long or curving at the top, continue to whip. However, overwhipping will cause the meringue to break. If the meringue starts looking chunky and starts to separate, that means it went past the stiff peaks point. If this happens, unfortunately you should dispose of the separated meringue and start again.

Add the food coloring, if you are using any.

Once the meringue has reached stiff peaks, pour the sifted dry ingredients into the bowl. If you are using any food coloring, add it at this point. Begin gently folding the dry ingredients with the meringue, forming the letter J with a rubber spatula by running it through the middle of the meringue and around the edges.

Begin stirring the batter with a spatula.

Fold the batter until it reaches the proper consistency.

The batter should be flowing off the spatula slowly and effortlessly.

You should be able to draw several figure eights with the batter that's flowing off the spatula.

The batter falling off the spatula quickly incorporates with the batter that's already in the bowl.

Once the dry ingredients and meringue are incorporated, I also like to squeeze some of the air out of the batter by using the spatula to press the batter against the sides of the bowl. Fold the batter until it has a lava consistency. That means the batter should be flowing slowly and effortlessly off the spatula. If you grab a spatula full of batter and hold it above the bowl, you should be able to draw several figure eights with the batter that flows off the spatula. And even after the batter breaks up, it should still continue to flow off the spatula. Also notice how the batter that's falling off the spatula is incorporating with the batter that's already in the bowl. They should be blending nicely together within 10 to 15 seconds.

(continued)

Transfer the batter to the piping bag.

You can use a bag tie to prevent the batter from drying or escaping from the top of the bag.

Once you achieve this stage, transfer the batter to a piping bag. Begin to pipe the shells onto a baking tray lined with a macaron mat by placing the bag about ¼ inch (6 mm) above the mat, 90 degrees over the center of each circle template. Apply gentle pressure for 3 to 5 seconds, then pull the bag up and twist at the top in a quick motion.

Pipe one full tray—20 to 30 macaron shells, depending on the size of the template on your macaron mat. Set the piping bag aside if you still have leftover batter. Bang the tray you've just piped against the counter six to eight times to release any air bubbles, or tap the bottom of the baking tray against your palm several times. Then use a toothpick to pop any remaining air bubbles on the surface of the macarons. It's important to do one tray at a time, and to pop the air bubbles immediately after piping—otherwise, your macarons will have holes in them if the air bubbles pop after the shells have started to dry out.

Once you are done piping, tapping and poking the bubbles of the first tray, move on to piping the remaining batter.

Let the trays rest for 20 to 40 minutes before baking. The drying time will depend on how humid your kitchen is, how much food coloring you've added to the batter, and on the overall consistency of the batter. Overmixed batters or batters made with a softer meringue may take longer to dry. Once you can touch the surface of a macaron with your fingers and it doesn't stick, they are ready to bake. If you live in a humid climate, be sure to turn on the air conditioning, if possible. If not, you can use a dehumidifier in the room where the macarons are resting, or let them dry near a fan, but do not have strong air blowing directly on the macarons.

Pipe at a 90-degree angle, applying gentle pressure to release the batter.

Use a toothpick to pop any remaining air bubbles.

Additionally, if the humidity is too high, it is better to skip letting the macarons rest at all, because they will end up absorbing the humidity from the air instead of drying. In this case, you can benefit from oven-drying the shells instead of air-drying them.

To dry the shells in the oven, simply preheat the oven to 325°F (160°C) as you make the batter. Then, right after piping the shells, place them in the oven and prop the door open about 4 inches (10 cm) and set a timer for 3 minutes. After the 3 minutes are up, close the oven door and let the macarons continue to bake until they are done, following the instructions in the next step. It's worth noting that a lot of people report having to turn their oven temperature down before using the oven-drying technique. Meanwhile, the rest of the batter should be resting inside the piping bag, waiting for the tray that is baking to finish before you pipe and bake the rest.

Bake one tray at a time for a total of 15 to 20 minutes. Unless it's super humid, as mentioned earlier, you should be fine to let the trays rest for as long as it takes to bake everything. Sometimes I even let my trays rest for over an hour if the macarons have a lot of food coloring in the batter.

Some bakers, including myself, have to rotate the trays 180 degrees in the oven after the first 5 minutes of baking. Whether or not you have to rotate the trays will depend on the heat distribution of your oven. If your macarons are coming out lopsided, or if random shells are cracking, you might benefit from rotating the trays as well.

To test if the macarons are done baking, try to wiggle one around. If it feels jiggly, it needs more time baking. Set your timer for another 3 to 5 minutes, and then check again. Once you wiggle a macaron and it feels firm, remove them from the oven. The macarons should have formed feet and a bottom skin, and shouldn't be gooey on the inside. You can also test by sacrificing one cookie and cracking it open to see how the inside is. If your macarons are browning too much while baking, cover them with a piece of foil or parchment paper. When I am baking white macarons, or lightly colored ones, I always cover them with a piece of foil after 8 minutes in the oven.

Remove the first tray from the oven and bake the second one. Let all of the macarons cool down completely before peeling them off the macaron mats and proceeding with the filling as instructed in whichever recipe you are following.

note: To make this a brown sugar macaron shell, simply substitute the same amount of granulated sugar for brown sugar, making sure there are no large lumps of brown sugar before adding it in. Adding brown sugar will give the shells a deeper and slightly nutty flavor, as well as a naturally tan color. Also keep in mind that the meringue might need about 2 more minutes of whipping than you are used to when using white sugar.

chocolate macaron shells

My second favorite macaron shells to make are chocolate-flavored ones. These go well with so many different filling flavors—caramel, Nutella®, coffee and, of course, more chocolate. A classic chocolate macaron shell is indispensable in your recipe repertoire, and once you nail it, you'll be able to create amazingly rich and indulgent treats.

yield: 40 (1½" [4-cm]) macaron shells

96 g almond flour

75 g powdered sugar, sifted

14 g cocoa powder

100 g granulated sugar

2 g egg white powder (optional)

100 g egg whites

Brown gel food coloring (optional, to deepen the color)

For detailed instructions, tips and tricks, refer to the Plain Macaron Shells recipe on page 24. This recipe follows the Plain Macaron Shells recipe, with the addition of cocoa powder to the dry ingredients, as well as a bit of brown gel food coloring to the meringue.

Preheat the oven to 325°F (160°C). Sift the almond flour, powdered sugar and cocoa powder into a bowl and set aside. Bring a pot of water to a low simmer over medium heat and place a heat-proof bowl on top. You can also use a double boiler if you prefer. The water shouldn't touch the bottom of the bowl.

Pour the granulated sugar and egg white powder (if using) into the heat-proof bowl and whisk together over the simmering water. Add the egg whites to the bowl and whisk the ingredients together for 2 to 4 minutes, until the sugar has completely melted. Wipe down the bottom of the bowl with a towel so that the water from the condensation doesn't drip into the meringue, then transfer the syrup to the bowl of a mixer.

Begin by whipping on low speed for 30 seconds. Increase the speed to medium-low for another 30 seconds, and then increase it to medium. Finish whipping on medium or medium-high until the meringue achieves stiff peaks.

Once the meringue is stiff, pour the sifted dry ingredients into the bowl. If you are using any food coloring, add it at this point. I like to add a touch of brown gel food coloring to deepen the color of these chocolate shells. Begin folding the dry ingredients with the meringue, forming the letter J with a rubber spatula by running it through the middle of the meringue and around the edges. Fold the batter until it has a lava consistency.

Once you achieve this stage, transfer the batter to a piping bag. Pipe one full tray, then set the bag aside if you still have leftover batter. Bang the tray you've just piped against the counter six to eight times to release any air bubbles, or tap the bottom of the baking tray against your palm several times. Then, use a toothpick to pop any remaining air bubbles on the surface of the macarons. Continue to pipe a second tray with any remaining batter.

Let the trays rest for 20 to 40 minutes before baking. Once you can touch the surface of a macaron with your fingers and it doesn't stick, you can bake.

Bake one tray at a time for a total of 15 to 20 minutes, until the shells are fully baked and no longer jiggly. Remove the first tray from the oven and bake the second one. Let all the macarons cool down before proceeding with the filling according to whichever recipe you are making.

coconut macaron shells

I'm often asked if coconut flour can be used when making coconut-flavored shells. The reason it can't be used to make macarons is because it absorbs a lot of liquid and simply won't work as successfully as almond flour. To flavor your macaron shells with coconut, the best alternative is to use coconut cream powder. Coconut cream powder is basically dried coconut milk—it has a highly concentrated coconut flavor and pairs fabulously with any fruity or chocolate fillings. I use these coconut shells in my Piña Colada Macarons recipe (page 87), among others.

yield: 40 (1½" [4-cm]) macaron shells

105 g almond flour

105 g powdered sugar, sifted

5 g coconut cream powder

100 g granulated sugar

4 g egg white powder (optional)

100 g egg whites

Gel-based food coloring of choice (optional)

For detailed instructions, tips and tricks, refer to the Plain Macaron Shells recipe on page 24. This recipe follows the Plain Macaron Shells recipe, with the addition of coconut cream powder to the dry ingredients, as well as any gel-based food coloring you desire to the meringue.

Preheat the oven to 325°F (160°C). Sift the almond flour, powdered sugar and coconut cream powder into a bowl and set aside. Bring a pot of water to a low simmer over medium heat and place a heat-proof bowl on top. You can also use a double boiler if you prefer. The water shouldn't touch the bottom of the bowl.

Pour the granulated sugar and egg white powder (if using) into the heat-proof bowl and whisk together over the simmering water. Add the egg whites to the bowl and whisk the ingredients together for 2 to 4 minutes, until the sugar has completely melted. Wipe down the bottom of the bowl with a towel so that the water from the condensation doesn't drip into the meringue, then transfer the syrup to the bowl of a mixer.

Begin by whipping on low speed for 30 seconds. Increase the speed to medium-low for another 30 seconds, and then increase it to medium. Finish whipping on medium or medium-high until the meringue achieves stiff peaks.

Once the meringue is stiff, pour the sifted dry ingredients into the bowl. If you are using any food coloring, add it at this point. Begin folding the dry ingredients with the meringue, forming the letter J with a rubber spatula by running it through the middle of the meringue and around the edges. Fold the batter until it has a lava consistency.

Once you achieve this stage, transfer the batter to a piping bag. Pipe one full tray, then set the bag aside if you still have leftover batter. Bang the tray you've just piped against the counter six to eight times to release any air bubbles, or tap the bottom of the baking tray against your palm several times. Then, use a toothpick to pop any remaining air bubbles on the surface of the macarons. Continue to pipe a second tray with any remaining batter.

Let the trays rest for 20 to 40 minutes before baking. Once you can touch the surface of a macaron with your fingers and it doesn't stick, you can bake.

Bake one tray at a time for a total of 15 to 20 minutes, until the shells are fully baked and no longer jiggly. Remove the first tray from the oven and bake the second one. Let all the macarons cool down before proceeding with the filling according to whichever recipe you are making.

lavender macaron shells

Lavender gives a delightful fragrance to these shells and adds a touch of elegance to any macaron. Be sure to use food-grade dried lavender, which can easily be found online. There are so many amazing ingredients that can be paired with lavender, including citrus, honey and even white chocolate. Lavender is truly unique and sure to elevate the flavor of your macarons. Its floral and almost minty taste can be very strong, so a little goes a long way and will be all you need to completely transform your macarons into an exquisite treat.

yield: 40 (1¹/₂" [4-cm]) macaron shells

2.5 g food-grade dried lavender buds
105 g almond flour
105 g powdered sugar, sifted
100 g granulated sugar
4 g egg white powder (optional)
100 g egg whites
Gel-based food coloring of choice (optional;
I like to use purple and blue tones in this recipe,
such as violet and periwinkle)

For detailed instructions, tips and tricks, refer to the Plain Macaron Shells recipe on page 24. This recipe follows the Plain Macaron Shells recipe, with the addition of ground lavender to the dry ingredients, as well as any gel-based food coloring you desire to the meringue.

Preheat the oven to 325°F (160°C).

Place the lavender buds in a coffee or spice grinder and pulse until the lavender turns into a powder.

Sift the almond flour, powdered sugar and lavender into a bowl and set it aside. Bring a pot of water to a low simmer over medium heat and place a heat-proof bowl on top. You can also use a double boiler if you prefer. The water shouldn't touch the bottom of the bowl.

Pour the granulated sugar and egg white powder (if using) into the heat-proof bowl and whisk together over the simmering water. Add the egg whites to the bowl and whisk the ingredients together for 2 to 4 minutes, until the sugar has completely melted. Wipe down the bottom of the bowl with a towel so that the water from the condensation doesn't drip into the meringue, then transfer the syrup to the bowl of a mixer.

Begin by whipping on low speed for 30 seconds. Increase the speed to medium-low for another 30 seconds, and then increase it to medium. Finish whipping on medium or medium-high until the meringue achieves stiff peaks.

Once the meringue is stiff, pour the sifted dry ingredients into the bowl. If you are using any food coloring, add it at this point. Begin folding the dry ingredients with the meringue, forming the letter J with a rubber spatula by running it through the middle of the meringue and around the edges. Fold the batter until it has a lava consistency.

Once you achieve this stage, transfer the batter to a piping bag. Pipe one full tray, then set the bag aside if you still have leftover batter. Bang the tray you've just piped against the counter six to eight times to release any air bubbles, or tap the bottom of the baking tray against your palm several times. Then, use a toothpick to pop any remaining air bubbles on the surface of the macarons. Continue to pipe a second tray with any remaining batter.

Let the trays rest for 20 to 40 minutes before baking. Once you can touch the surface of a macaron with your fingers and it doesn't stick, you can bake.

Bake one tray at a time for a total of 15 to 20 minutes, until the shells are fully baked and no longer jiggly. Remove the first tray from the oven and bake the second one. Let all the macarons cool down before proceeding with the filling according to whichever recipe you are making.

matcha macaron shells

This was the first flavored macaron recipe I ever published on my blog, Pies and Tacos, and it is still one of my most popular recipes years later. Matcha macarons are highly requested by my friends, probably because of their distinct flavor, smooth finish and subtle bittersweetness. Matcha can be paired with berries, white chocolate, vanilla, almond, peanut butter and so many other flavors. The Matcha Blueberry Macarons recipe (page 85) is one of my favorites, and it's one of the first I developed for this book.

yield: 40 (1½" [4-cm]) macaron shells

105 g almond flour
105 g powdered sugar, sifted
3 g matcha powder
100 g granulated sugar
2 g egg white powder (optional)
100 g egg whites
Green gel food coloring (optional)

For detailed instructions, tips and tricks, refer to the Plain Macaron Shells recipe on page 24. This recipe follows the Plain Macaron Shells recipe, with the addition of matcha powder to the dry ingredients, as well as a bit of green gel food coloring to the meringue.

Preheat the oven to 325°F (160°C). Sift the almond flour, powdered sugar and matcha powder into a bowl and set it aside. Bring a pot of water to a low simmer over medium heat and place a heat-proof bowl on top. You can also use a double boiler if you prefer. The water shouldn't touch the bottom of the bowl.

Pour the granulated sugar and egg white powder (if using) into the heat-proof bowl and whisk together over the simmering water. Add the egg whites to the bowl and whisk the ingredients together for 2 to 4 minutes, until the sugar has completely melted. Wipe down the bottom of the bowl with a towel so that the water from the condensation doesn't drip into the meringue, then transfer the syrup to the bowl of a mixer.

Begin by whipping on low speed for 30 seconds. Increase the speed to medium-low for another 30 seconds, and then increase it to medium. Finish whipping on medium or medium-high until the meringue achieves stiff peaks.

Once the meringue is stiff, pour the sifted dry ingredients into the bowl. If you are using any food coloring, add it at this point. I like to add a bit of green gel food coloring to the batter. Begin folding the dry ingredients with the meringue, forming the letter J with a rubber spatula by running it through the middle of the meringue and around the edges. Fold the batter until it has a lava consistency.

Once you achieve this stage, transfer the batter to a piping bag. Pipe one full tray, then set the bag aside if you still have leftover batter. Bang the tray you've just piped against the counter six to eight times to release any air bubbles, or tap the bottom of the baking tray against your palm several times. Then, use a toothpick to pop any remaining air bubbles on the surface of the macarons. Continue to pipe a second tray with any remaining batter.

Let the trays rest for 20 to 40 minutes before baking. Once you can touch the surface of a macaron with your fingers and it doesn't stick, you can bake.

Bake one tray at a time for a total of 15 to 20 minutes, until the shells are fully baked and no longer jiggly. Remove the first tray from the oven and bake the second one. Let all the macarons cool down before proceeding with the filling according to whichever recipe you are making.

spiced macaron shells

When adding spices to macaron shells, you should only need to use $1/4$ to $1/2$ teaspoon (up to 1 gram). You can certainly experiment by adding a bit more, but that's as much as I like to add. I always prefer to focus on making the filling of the macarons shine, but adding a bit of spice to the shells can create another layer of flavor and heighten the whole experience.

A few spices to try include cinnamon, cardamom, chai, ginger, cloves, nutmeg and pumpkin spice, which are all great on their own, but feel free to experiment with different spice mixes to discover what you like best! To add spices to the macaron batter, simply sift them along with the dry ingredients—almond flour and powdered sugar—or sprinkle them over the shells before baking. You can also use vanilla bean, if you'd like. If using vanilla bean to flavor your shells, add the scraped seeds from half a vanilla bean pod.

yield: 40 (1$1/2$" [4-cm]) macaron shells

105 g almond flour

105 g powdered sugar, sifted

Up to 1 g ($1/4$–$1/2$ tsp) spices, or $1/2$ vanilla bean

100 g granulated sugar

4 g egg white powder (optional)

100 g egg whites

Gel-based food coloring of choice (optional)

For detailed instructions, tips and tricks, refer to the Plain Macaron Shells recipe on page 24. This recipe follows the Plain Macaron Shells recipe, with the addition of spices or vanilla bean seeds to the dry ingredients, as well as any gel-based food coloring you desire to the meringue.

Preheat the oven to 325°F (160°C). Sift the almond flour, powdered sugar and any spices you might be using into a bowl and set it aside. If you are using half of a vanilla bean, simply scrape the seeds into the bowl with the other dry ingredients. Bring a pot of water to a low simmer over medium heat and place a heat-proof bowl on top. You can also use a double boiler if you prefer. The water shouldn't touch the bottom of the bowl.

Pour the granulated sugar and egg white powder (if using) into the heat-proof bowl and whisk together over the simmering water. Add the egg whites to the bowl and whisk the ingredients together for 2 to 4 minutes, until the sugar has completely melted. Wipe down the bottom of the bowl with a towel so that the water from the condensation doesn't drip into the meringue, then transfer the syrup to the bowl of a mixer.

Begin by whipping on low speed for 30 seconds. Increase the speed to medium-low for another 30 seconds, and then increase it to medium. Finish whipping on medium or medium-high until the meringue achieves stiff peaks.

Once the meringue is stiff, pour the sifted dry ingredients into the bowl. If you are using any food coloring, add it at this point. Begin folding the dry ingredients with the meringue, forming the letter J with a rubber spatula by running it through the middle of the meringue and around the edges. Fold the batter until it has a lava consistency.

Once you achieve this stage, transfer the batter to a piping bag. Pipe one full tray, then set the bag aside if you still have leftover batter. Bang the tray you've just piped against the counter six to eight times to release any air bubbles, or tap the bottom of the baking tray against your palm several times. Then, use a toothpick to pop any remaining air bubbles on the surface of the macarons. Continue to pipe a second tray with any remaining batter.

Let the trays rest for 20 to 40 minutes before baking. Once you can touch the surface of a macaron with your fingers and it doesn't stick, you can bake.

Bake one tray at a time for a total of 15 to 20 minutes, until the shells are fully baked and no longer jiggly. Remove the first tray from the oven and bake the second one. Let all the macarons cool down before proceeding with the filling according to whichever recipe you are making.

coffee macaron shells

If you love coffee and are looking to make a coffee-flavored macaron, try adding a bit of espresso powder to the shells. You could use regular coffee grounds instead, as long as they are as fine as espresso powder. That being said, you may still want to be careful, as espresso powder is usually a lot finer and has a stronger coffee taste than regular coffee grounds. Plus, regular coffee grounds might not dissolve fully in the batter.

yield: 40 (1½" [4-cm]) macaron shells

105 g almond flour
105 g powdered sugar, sifted
1 g (½ tsp) espresso powder
100 g granulated sugar
4 g egg white powder (optional)
100 g egg whites
Gel-based food coloring of choice (optional; I like to use a brown color in this recipe)

For detailed instructions, tips and tricks, refer to the Plain Macaron Shells recipe on page 24. This recipe follows the Plain Macaron Shells recipe, with the addition of espresso powder to the dry ingredients, as well as any gel-based food coloring you desire to the meringue.

Preheat the oven to 325°F (160°C). Sift the almond flour, powdered sugar and espresso powder into a bowl and set it aside. Bring a pot of water to a low simmer over medium heat and place a heat-proof bowl on top. You can also use a double boiler if you prefer. The water shouldn't touch the bottom of the bowl.

Pour the granulated sugar and egg white powder (if using) into the heat-proof bowl and whisk together over the simmering water. Add the egg whites to the bowl and whisk the ingredients together for 2 to 4 minutes, until the sugar has completely melted. Wipe down the bottom of the bowl with a towel so that the water from the condensation doesn't drip into the meringue, then transfer the syrup to the bowl of a mixer.

Begin by whipping on low speed for 30 seconds. Increase the speed to medium-low for another 30 seconds, and then increase it to medium. Finish whipping on medium or medium-high until the meringue achieves stiff peaks.

Once the meringue is stiff, pour the sifted dry ingredients into the bowl. If you are using any food coloring, add it at this point. Begin folding the dry ingredients with the meringue, forming the letter J with a rubber spatula by running it through the middle of the meringue and around the edges. Fold the batter until it has a lava consistency.

Once you achieve this stage, transfer the batter to a piping bag. Pipe one full tray, then set the bag aside if you still have leftover batter. Bang the tray you've just piped against the counter six to eight times to release any air bubbles, or tap the bottom of the baking tray against your palm several times. Then, use a toothpick to pop any remaining air bubbles on the surface of the macarons. Continue to pipe a second tray with any remaining batter.

Let the trays rest for 20 to 40 minutes before baking. Once you can touch the surface of a macaron with your fingers and it doesn't stick, you can bake.

Bake one tray at a time for a total of 15 to 20 minutes, until the shells are fully baked and no longer jiggly. Remove the first tray from the oven and bake the second one. Let all the macarons cool down before proceeding with the filling according to whichever recipe you are making.

freeze-dried fruit macaron shells

Using freeze-dried fruit powder is a great way to flavor macaron shells. It works especially well for flavors like strawberry and raspberry, but other flavors can be a bit more subtle, such as banana and mango.

I don't recommend using more than the 5 grams of freeze-dried fruit powder listed here for each 100 grams of egg whites, as it can dry up the macaron batter, making it stiff and hard to stir. Also note that I reduce the amount of powdered sugar in this recipe to compensate for the added freeze-dried powder, which will also help keep the batter from becoming too stiff.

If you can only find whole freeze-dried fruit pieces, simply process about 8 grams of the fruit pieces in a small blender. Then, sift the powder obtained to eliminate any large chunks. You may need to process a bit more than 5 grams in order to obtain 5 grams of powder for the recipe, which is why I am instructing you to process 8 grams.

yield: 40 (1½" [4-cm]) macaron shells

105 g almond flour

100 g powdered sugar, sifted

5 g freeze-dried fruit powder (such as strawberry, raspberry or banana)

100 g white granulated sugar

2 g egg white powder (optional)

100 g egg whites

Gel-based food coloring of choice (optional)

For detailed instructions, tips and tricks, refer to the Plain Macaron Shells recipe on page 24. This recipe follows the Plain Macaron Shells recipe, with the addition of freeze-dried fruit powder to the dry ingredients, as well as any gel-based food coloring you desire to the meringue.

Preheat the oven to 325°F (160°C). Sift the almond flour, powdered sugar and freeze-dried fruit powder into a bowl and set it aside. Bring a pot of water to a low simmer over medium heat and place a heat-proof bowl on top. You can also use a double boiler if you prefer. The water shouldn't touch the bottom of the bowl.

Pour the granulated sugar and egg white powder (if using) into the heat-proof bowl and whisk together over the simmering water. Add the egg whites to the bowl and whisk the ingredients together for 2 to 4 minutes, until the sugar has completely melted. Wipe down the bottom of the bowl with a towel so that the water from the condensation doesn't drip into the meringue, then transfer the syrup to the bowl of a mixer.

Begin by whipping on low speed for 30 seconds. Increase the speed to medium-low for another 30 seconds, and then increase it to medium. Finish whipping on medium or medium-high until the meringue achieves stiff peaks.

Once the meringue is stiff, pour the sifted dry ingredients into the bowl. If you are using any food coloring, add it at this point. Begin folding the dry ingredients with the meringue, forming the letter J with a rubber spatula by running it through the middle of the meringue and around the edges. Fold the batter until it has a lava consistency.

Once you achieve this stage, transfer the batter to a piping bag. Pipe one full tray, then set the bag aside if you still have leftover batter. Bang the tray you've just piped against the counter six to eight times to release any air bubbles, or tap the bottom of the baking tray against your palm several times. Then, use a toothpick to pop any remaining air bubbles on the surface of the macarons. Continue to pipe a second tray with any remaining batter.

Let the trays rest for 20 to 40 minutes before baking. Once you can touch the surface of a macaron with your fingers and it doesn't stick, you can bake.

Bake one tray at a time for a total of 15 to 20 minutes, until the shells are fully baked and no longer jiggly. Remove the first tray from the oven and bake the second one. Let all the macarons cool down before proceeding with the filling according to whichever recipe you are making.

citrus zest
macaron shells

Adding dried citrus zest to the macaron batter will give your shells a delicious aroma. To ensure your batter turns out well, use zest that is dry and finely minced. If the zest is too chunky, it will form bumps or even cracks in the macaron shells. I recommend using a microplane or a zester to obtain a fine zest, and I suggest staying away from graters that will yield a chunky zest.

The best zest I've tried so far was lime. It gave the shells an outstanding zesty flavor, but feel free to experiment with different zests. Do keep in mind that orange and grapefruit zest might not be as flavorful and won't make a big difference in the taste of the shells.

yield: 40 (1½" [4-cm]) macaron shells

2 g citrus zest (lime or lemon)
105 g almond flour
100 g powdered sugar, sifted
100 g white granulated sugar
4 g egg white powder (optional)
100 g egg whites
Gel-based food coloring of choice (optional)

For detailed instructions, tips and tricks, refer to the Plain Macaron Shells recipe on page 24. This recipe follows the Plain Macaron Shells recipe, with the addition of dried powdered zest to the dry ingredients, as well as any gel-based food coloring you desire to the meringue.

Zest 1 large or 2 small lemons or limes. Place the zest on a small plate or dish lined with wax paper. Cover the zest loosely and let it sit on the counter for at least 6 hours, maybe longer, until completely dry to the touch. Then, place it in a small blender or coffee grinder and process briefly, just until the zest has a powdery consistency.

Preheat the oven to 325°F (160°C). Sift the almond flour, powdered sugar and zest powder into a bowl and set it aside. Bring a pot of water to a low simmer over medium heat and place a heat-proof bowl on top. You can also use a double boiler if you prefer. The water shouldn't touch the bottom of the bowl.

Pour the granulated sugar and egg white powder (if using) into the heat-proof bowl and whisk together over the simmering water. Add the egg whites to the bowl and whisk the ingredients together for 2 to 4 minutes, until the sugar has completely melted. Wipe down the bottom of the bowl with a towel so that the water from the condensation doesn't drip into the meringue, then transfer the syrup to the bowl of a mixer.

Begin by whipping on low speed for 30 seconds. Increase the speed to medium-low for another 30 seconds, and then increase it to medium. Finish whipping on medium or medium-high until the meringue achieves stiff peaks.

Once the meringue is stiff, pour the sifted dry ingredients into the bowl. If you are using any food coloring, add it at this point. Begin folding the dry ingredients with the meringue, forming the letter J with a rubber spatula by running it through the middle of the meringue and around the edges. Fold the batter until it has a lava consistency.

Once you achieve this stage, transfer the batter to a piping bag. Pipe one full tray, then set the bag aside if you still have leftover batter. Bang the tray you've just piped against the counter 6 to 8 times to release any air bubbles, or tap the bottom of the baking tray against your palm several times. Then, use a toothpick to pop any remaining air bubbles on the surface of the macarons. Continue to pipe a second tray with any remaining batter.

Let the trays rest for 20 to 40 minutes before baking. Once you can touch the surface of a macaron with your fingers and it doesn't stick, you can bake.

Bake one tray at a time for a total of 15 to 20 minutes, until the shells are fully baked and no longer jiggly. Remove the first tray from the oven and bake the second one. Let all the macarons cool down before proceeding with the filling according to whichever recipe you are making.

pistachio macaron shells

Pistachio macarons are always noteworthy. The ground pistachios add a deliciously sweet and buttery pistachio taste to the shells. I recommend using raw pistachios or dry-roasted pistachios to make the pistachio flour for the shells. Don't use oil-roasted pistachios, as the oils will affect the macaron batter. If using raw pistachios, you also have the option to blanch them in order to obtain a green flour. The dry-roasted pistachios can't be blanched and will make for a flour that is brown in color, but delicious nevertheless, though you can also use green gel food coloring to make the shells green.

yield: 40 (1½" [4-cm]) macaron shells

pistachio flour
40 g pistachios

macaron shells
80 g almond flour
28 g pistachio flour
100 g powdered sugar, sifted
100 g white granulated sugar
4 g egg white powder (optional)
100 g egg whites
Green gel food coloring (optional)

For detailed instructions, tips and tricks, refer to the Plain Macaron Shells recipe on page 24. This recipe follows the Plain Macaron Shells recipe, with the addition of pistachio flour to the dry ingredients, as well as green gel food coloring to the meringue.

The amount of pistachios you will need to obtain 28 grams of flour can vary due to the amount of oils released during processing. That being said, 40 grams of pistachios is usually enough to get you there, though it can be helpful to have extra pistachios on hand, just in case.

To make the pistachio flour from raw, shelled pistachios, you can blanch them a day in advance to remove the skins. First, bring a medium pot of water to a boil. Meanwhile, place a medium bowl filled with ice water next to the pot of water, and line a baking sheet with paper towels. Add the pistachios to the boiling water. After 2 minutes, remove the pistachios using a slotted spoon and immediately place them in the ice water bath.

After a couple of minutes, remove the pistachios from the cold bath and spread them out on the prepared baking sheet. Use a clean kitchen towel or another paper towel to rub the pistachios, which will help the skins come off. Then, pick each pistachio, one by one, removing and discarding the skins.

Let the pistachios air-dry on the baking tray overnight.

The next day, once they are fully dry, place them in the food processor. If you are using dry-roasted pistachios, you can skip the whole blanching process and start the recipe from this point. Process the pistachios 10 to 20 times, then stop and sift the pistachios into a bowl. You will still have a lot of large pieces of pistachios in the sifter. Return them to the food processor and repeat. Process about 10 times and sift again. The number of times you process can depend on how powerful your food processor is. Be very careful not to overprocess the pistachios, as this will cause them to release oils and turn into butter. This is why it's so important to process a bit at a time, to filter out the pistachio that's already ground and prevent them from releasing oils.

This is why I am calling for a larger amount of pistachios than what you will need for the macaron batter. It's very hard to obtain 100 percent finely ground flour from processing the pistachios. Some of it will be larger pieces, and if you continue to grind them, they will turn into butter. You can use the extra pistachio pieces to decorate the tops of the finished macarons or simply add them to the buttercream filling.

Once you measure out 28 grams of flour, you can stop processing the pistachios. And always make sure to stop processing before it begins to release oils and turn into butter.

Preheat the oven to 325°F (160°C). Sift the almond flour, powdered sugar and pistachio flour into a bowl and set it aside. Bring a pot of water to a low simmer over medium heat and place a heat-proof bowl on top. You can also use a double boiler if you prefer. The water shouldn't touch the bottom of the bowl.

Pour the granulated sugar and egg white powder (if using) into the heat-proof bowl and whisk together over the simmering water. Add the egg whites to the bowl and whisk the ingredients together for 2 to 4 minutes, until the sugar has completely melted. Wipe down the bottom of the bowl with a towel so that the water from the condensation doesn't drip into the meringue, then transfer the syrup to the bowl of a mixer.

Begin by whipping on low speed for 30 seconds. Increase the speed to medium-low for another 30 seconds, and then increase it to medium. Finish whipping on medium or medium-high until the meringue achieves stiff peaks.

Once the meringue is stiff, pour the sifted dry ingredients into the bowl. If you are using any food coloring, add it at this point. I like to add green gel food coloring to make the shells a deeper, more vibrant green. Begin folding the dry ingredients with the meringue, forming the letter J with a rubber spatula by running it through the middle of the meringue and around the edges. Fold the batter until it has a lava consistency.

Once you achieve this stage, transfer the batter to a piping bag. Pipe one full tray, then set the bag aside if you still have leftover batter. Bang the tray you've just piped against the counter 6 to 8 times to release any air bubbles, or tap the bottom of the baking tray against your palm several times. Then use a toothpick to pop any remaining air bubbles on the surface of the macarons. Continue to pipe a second tray with any remaining batter.

Let the trays rest for 20 to 40 minutes before baking. Once you can touch the surface of a macaron with your fingers and it doesn't stick, you can bake.

Bake one tray at a time for a total of 15 to 20 minutes, until the shells are fully baked and no longer jiggly. Remove the first tray from the oven and bake the second one. Let all the macarons cool down before proceeding with the filling according to whichever recipe you are making.

rich and decadent

In this chapter, get ready to embark on a journey to the land of outrageously rich and indulgent macaron flavors. Many of my favorite macarons from the book are in this chapter, including the Fleur de Sel Caramel Macarons (page 43), Brownie Batter Macarons (page 45), Caramel S'mores Macarons (page 60) and Dalgona Coffee Macarons (page 56). The flavors in this chapter are bold, intense and luscious—perfect to enjoy with a tall glass of milk.

fleur de sel caramel macarons

Salted caramel is a classic macaron flavor that should never be missing from your repertoire. The most famous macaron baker in the world, Pierre Hermé, was the inventor of salted caramel, and here we honor him with this splendid recipe. Fleur de sel is an exquisite, light, flaky sea salt that is totally worth the investment. It adds a high-quality flavor to the macarons, but if you can't find it, other coarse salts or finishing salts will also work. Because of its high butter content, the caramel is so thick that it can hold its own as a filling. The flavor layering provided by the addition of salt makes these slightly salty, buttery and sweet macarons a huge hit with whoever tries them.

yield: 20 (1½" [4-cm]) macaron sandwiches

1 batch Plain Macaron Shells (page 24) dyed with a few drops of sky blue gel food coloring

fleur de sel caramel sauce

¼ cup (60 ml) water

¾ cup (150 g) granulated sugar

½ cup (120 ml) heavy cream

11½ tbsp (161 g) unsalted butter, at room temperature

1 tsp fleur de sel, or coarse sea salt, plus more for sprinkling

tools

Candy thermometer

2 piping bags

Round piping tip (½" [1.3 cm] in diameter) or piping tip of your choice

First, make the Plain Macaron Shells by following the directions on page 24, adding sky blue gel food coloring to the batter when instructed.

Before making the Fleur de Sel Caramel Sauce, make sure all of the ingredients are measured out and ready to go. In a pan with a heavy bottom, begin by combining the water and sugar over medium heat, mixing until they are incorporated. Use a basting brush dipped in water to brush the sides of the pan and dissolve any stray sugar crystals.

Place a candy thermometer on the side of the pan, and let the syrup come to a boil, undisturbed. Slowly, it will start to darken. Once the syrup reaches about 340°F (171°C) and has a deep amber color, remove it from the heat. It should take 20 to 25 minutes to reach this temperature, but the time frame will depend on how strong the heat is. Be very careful at this point, because the caramel can be seconds away from burning and becoming bitter, so you have to act fast. This is why it's important to have all of the ingredients ready to go before getting started.

Pour the cream over the amber-colored syrup. Be very careful as you pour, because the mixture will bubble up fiercely. Wear heat-resistant gloves or keep your hands away from the top of the pan to prevent burning yourself.

After a few seconds, the foam and bubbles will subside a bit. Once this happens, place the pan back on the stove over low heat.

The cream and sugar should be incorporated and bubbling gently at this point. If any bits of sugar are still crystallized, just continue to stir for another 10 seconds or so until they melt. Always be careful to not overcook the caramel, or it will harden up too much as it cools down later.

(continued)

fleur de sel caramel macarons (continued)

Add the butter to the pan, a couple of tablespoons (28 g) at a time, stirring between each addition. Once all of the butter has been added, add the fleur de sel and mix to combine. Then, remove the caramel from the heat. It will be very hot and runny, so pour it into a heat-proof bowl and let it cool down to room temperature. Then, cover the bowl and place it in the fridge overnight.

The next day, line a piping bag with a piping tip. Place the Fleur de Sel Caramel Sauce in the piping bag, and pipe it onto the shells. Another alternative is to whip the caramel for a couple of minutes with an electric mixer on medium-high speed to make it thicker and lighter in color. Be sure to reserve some unwhipped caramel sauce for decorating the tops of the macarons later. I like it best unwhipped, but that's a personal preference and will also depend on the consistency of your caramel. If for some reason your caramel turned out too runny, whipping can make it thicker.

To assemble the macarons, pipe a small amount of caramel sauce on each bottom macaron shell, then top with another shell.

To decorate the macarons, place some of the unwhipped caramel sauce in a piping bag, and snip the end with scissors. Then, pipe a drizzle of caramel on top of the macarons and sprinkle salt on top.

Let the macarons chill, covered, in the fridge overnight before serving, then let them sit at room temperature for 10 to 20 minutes before enjoying.

The Fleur de Sel Caramel Macarons will store well, covered, in the fridge for up to 5 days, or in the freezer, in an airtight container, for up to a month.

brownie batter macarons

I am not trying to play favorites, but there's no way around it—these Brownie Batter Macarons are one of my best creations! They are filled with Edible Brownie Batter and the silkiest Chocolate Pudding Frosting. Each bite will leave you wishing for more. These macarons are rich and indulgent and will satisfy all of your chocolatey sweet-tooth cravings.

yield: 20 (1½" [4-cm]) macaron sandwiches

1 batch Chocolate Macaron Shells (page 30)

edible brownie batter

3 tbsp (32 g) chocolate chips
1 tbsp (14 g) unsalted butter
¼ cup (50 g) brown sugar
3 tbsp (21 g) almond flour
1 tbsp (8 g) cocoa powder
Pinch of salt
¼ tsp vanilla extract

chocolate pudding frosting

1 tbsp (15 ml) heavy cream
2½ tbsp (28 g) chocolate chips or chopped chocolate
6 tbsp (85 g) unsalted butter, at room temperature
½ cup (63 g) powdered sugar, sifted, plus more as needed
3 tbsp (24 g) cocoa powder
½ tsp vanilla extract

topping

½ cup (85 g) chopped chocolate
¼ cup (38 g) chocolate crispearls

tools

2 piping bags
Open star piping tip (¼" [6 mm] in diameter) or piping tip of your choice

First, make the Chocolate Macaron Shells by following the directions on page 30.

Line a piping bag with a piping tip to pipe the Chocolate Pudding Frosting onto the shells. Set aside.

To make the Edible Brownie Batter, place the chocolate chips and butter in a small heat-proof bowl and microwave the mixture for 10-second intervals, stirring in between, until completely melted. Once the chocolate and the butter have melted together, add the brown sugar, almond flour, cocoa powder, salt and vanilla to the bowl and stir until a dough is formed. Keep the brownie batter covered until ready to use.

To make the Chocolate Pudding Frosting, heat the cream gently in a small bowl in the microwave for about 15 seconds, until hot. Place the chocolate chips in a separate bowl and pour the hot cream over it, then stir until melted. If the chocolate doesn't melt completely, place the mixture in the microwave for 5-second intervals, stirring in between, until completely melted. Be careful not to overheat the chocolate.

(continued)

Once the chocolate has fully melted, let it cool down for about 15 minutes until it comes to room temperature. If the chocolate is warmer than room temperature, the frosting will be soupy and runny.

When the chocolate is at room temperature, beat the butter in a separate bowl with a mixer for 1 to 2 minutes, until creamy. Turn the mixer off, and add the powdered sugar and cocoa powder to the butter, along with the melted chocolate mixture. Mix on low speed until the ingredients are incorporated, then raise the speed to medium-high and beat for about 2 minutes until a creamy and smooth frosting forms. Add the vanilla and mix to combine. If the frosting is too runny, add more powdered sugar, only a couple of tablespoons (16 g) at a time until you achieve the proper consistency. Transfer the frosting to the prepared piping bag.

To decorate the top shells, place the chocolate in a small heat-proof bowl and microwave it for 15-second intervals, stirring in between, until completely melted. Dip the tops of 20 shells in the melted chocolate, then place them in the fridge for 10 minutes to dry. Once the chocolate on top of the shells has set, place the remaining chocolate that was left in the bowl in a piping bag, and snip the end with scissors. You may have to remelt the chocolate if it sat for too long. Then, drizzle it over the dry macaron shells. Top with the chocolate crispearls.

To assemble the macarons, pipe a ring of Chocolate Pudding Frosting around the edges of each bottom shell. Then, spoon some of the Edible Brownie Batter in the center of each macaron. Top with a decorated shell.

Let the macarons chill, covered, in the fridge overnight before serving, then let them sit at room temperature for 10 to 20 minutes before enjoying.

The Brownie Batter Macarons will store well, covered, in the fridge for up to 5 days, or in the freezer, in an airtight container, for up to a month.

sticky toffee macarons

The name says it all: These macarons are sticky and finger-licking delicious! The Date Caramel Sauce is made out of dates and golden syrup—the same way we make caramel sauce for sticky toffee pudding, which is the dessert that inspired this macaron flavor. The shells are made with brown sugar instead of white for a deep caramel flavor with nutty notes. These delicious Sticky Toffee Macarons will be in great company with a hot cup of coffee or Earl Grey tea.

yield: 20 (1½" [4-cm]) macaron sandwiches

1 batch Plain Macaron Shells (page 24) made with brown sugar instead of granulated sugar

date caramel sauce

1 cup (177 g) Medjool dates
⅓ cup (78 ml) golden syrup
¼ cup (60 ml) whole milk
½ tsp vanilla extract

date caramel buttercream

6 tbsp (85 g) unsalted butter, at room temperature
¼ cup (60 ml) Date Caramel Sauce
2 cups (250 g) powdered sugar, sifted, plus more as needed
1 tsp vanilla extract
Milk or cream, as needed (optional)

for decoration

¼ cup (38 g) caramel crispearls

tools

2 piping bags
Round piping tip (¼" [6 mm] in diameter) or piping tip of your choice

First, make the Plain Macaron Shells by following the directions on page 24, substituting the granulated sugar in the recipe with brown sugar.

Line a piping bag with a piping tip to pipe the Date Caramel Buttercream onto the shells. Set aside.

To make the Date Caramel Sauce, begin by soaking the dates in a bowl with warm water for about 10 minutes—or up to an hour if they are super dry—until they become soft and hydrated. After soaking, remove the skin and the seeds of each date.

Place the dates in a small blender or food processor. Add the golden syrup, milk and vanilla, and process the mixture for 1 minute until smooth. Scrape down the sides of the blender, and process the mixture again for another 30 seconds to 1 minute, until there are no large bits of dates in the sauce.

To make the Date Caramel Buttercream, begin by beating the butter in a large bowl with an electric mixer for 1 to 2 minutes, until creamy. Add ¼ cup (60 ml) of the Date Caramel Sauce, and beat for 30 seconds to combine.

Add the powdered sugar to the bowl, and beat the mixture for another minute until creamy and incorporated, scraping the sides if necessary. Add the vanilla and mix to incorporate. If the buttercream is too stiff, add 1 teaspoon of milk or cream. If the buttercream is too soft and runny, add more powdered sugar, a couple of tablespoons (16 g) at a time, until you achieve the proper consistency. Transfer the buttercream to the prepared piping bag.

To assemble the macarons, pipe a ring of buttercream around the edges of each bottom macaron shell. Fill the middle of the buttercream ring with the Date Caramel Sauce. Then, top with another shell.

To decorate the macarons, place some of the leftover Date Caramel Sauce in a piping bag and snip the end with scissors, then pipe two lines crosswise on top of the macarons and top with caramel crispearls.

Let the macarons chill, covered, in the fridge overnight before serving, then let them sit at room temperature for 10 to 20 minutes before enjoying.

The Sticky Toffee Macarons will store well, covered, in the fridge for up to 5 days, or in the freezer, in an airtight container, for up to a month.

chili hot chocolate macarons

Chocolate and chili peppers are two gifts from Mexico to the world, and their pairing can be attributed to the ancient Mayans. Here, chocolate and cayenne pepper come together in the form of delicious macarons. The cayenne pepper in the Fudge Filling won't make the macarons spicy; rather, it will simply leave a delectable lingering taste in your mouth after each bite. This is a very exhilarating flavor combo that's worth exploring. The Marshmallow Frosting surrounding the fudge center is the perfect complement to the Fudge Filling because it doesn't take away from the richness of the chocolate and chili combo—it simply adds another gooey layer of texture and sweetness to make the experience even more delightful.

yield: 20 (1¹/₂" [4-cm]) macaron sandwiches

1 batch Chocolate Macaron Shells (page 30)

fudge filling
3 tbsp (37 g) granulated sugar
3 tbsp (45 ml) heavy cream
3 tbsp (24 g) cocoa powder
3 tbsp (42 g) unsalted butter
Pinch of cayenne pepper

marshmallow frosting
2 egg whites (30 g)
¹/₂ cup (100 g) granulated sugar
¹/₄ tsp cream of tartar
¹/₈ tsp fine sea salt
1 tsp vanilla extract

for decoration
¹/₂ cup (85 g) chopped chocolate
¹/₃ cup (19 g) dehydrated mini marshmallows
¹/₄ cup (38 g) chocolate crispearls

tools
Piping bag
Round piping tip (¹/₄" [6 mm] in diameter) or piping tip of your choice
Candy thermometer

First, make the Chocolate Macaron Shells by following the directions on page 30.

Line a piping bag with a piping tip to pipe the Marshmallow Frosting onto the shells. Set aside.

To make the Fudge Filling, heat the sugar, cream, cocoa powder and butter in a small saucepan over medium heat. Bring the mixture to a low simmer, stirring constantly for about 4 minutes until all the ingredients have combined to form a smooth sauce. Remove the filling from the heat, add the cayenne pepper and stir to combine. Let the filling cool completely to room temperature before using it to fill the macarons. If you store it in the fridge, you can reheat it gently in the microwave for a few seconds and stir until smooth. Only use the sauce when it's at room temperature—it shouldn't be either hot or cold.

To make the Marshmallow Frosting, combine the egg whites, sugar, cream of tartar and salt in a heat-proof bowl. Set the bowl over a pot of barely simmering water to form a double boiler. Make sure the bottom of the bowl isn't touching the water, to prevent the whites from cooking.

(continued)

Whisk the mixture for a few minutes until it reaches 140°F (60°C) on a candy thermometer. Once the syrup is to temperature, remove the bowl from the double boiler. Whip the syrup with an electric mixer fitted with a whisk attachment for about 5 minutes on high speed. Add the vanilla and mix to combine. By this point, the meringue should have firm peaks and be fluffy and glossy. If not, continue to whip, as some mixers might take longer to get there. Transfer the frosting to the prepared piping bag. The Marshmallow Frosting has to be piped immediately after being made. It will hold up nicely after it is piped, but if you don't pipe it right away, it will begin to deflate and become runny.

To assemble the macarons, pipe a ring of Marshmallow Frosting around the edges of each bottom shell. Spoon a bit of Fudge Filling in the center of each macaron. Top with another shell.

To decorate the macarons, place the chocolate in a heat-proof bowl, and microwave it for 15-second intervals, stirring in between, until the chocolate is completely melted. Dip half of each macaron sandwich in the melted chocolate, and then place it on a baking sheet lined with parchment or silicone, for easy removal later. Top the macarons with dehydrated mini marshmallows and crispearls.

Let the macarons chill, covered, in the fridge overnight before serving, then let them sit at room temperature for 10 to 20 minutes before enjoying.

The Chili Hot Chocolate Macarons will store well, covered, in the fridge for up to 5 days, or in the freezer, in an airtight container, for up to a month.

caramel macchiato macarons

This crowd-pleasing flavor combination of coffee and caramel is a major hit! Espresso-flavored macaron shells are filled with a smooth and velvety Salted Caramel Sauce surrounded by an indulgent, creamy Caramel Coffee Buttercream. These macarons have a proper kick of caffeine and a delightful caramel sweetness with hints of vanilla. They make me think about the simple pleasures in life: being in a coffee shop, listening to jazz music and enjoying a treat and a cup of coffee.

yield: 20 (1½" [4-cm]) macaron sandwiches

1 batch Coffee Macaron Shells (page 35) made using the Multicolored Shells technique for two-tone macarons demonstrated on page 148. Dye half the batter with brown gel food coloring, and leave the other half undyed.

salted caramel sauce

½ cup (100 g) granulated sugar
¼ cup (60 ml) heavy cream
2½ tbsp (35 g) unsalted butter
¼ tsp kosher salt
½ tsp vanilla extract

caramel coffee buttercream

6 tbsp (85 g) unsalted butter, at room temperature
¼ cup (60 ml) Salted Caramel Sauce, at room temperature
1½ cups (188 g) powdered sugar, sifted
1 tsp espresso powder
1 tsp Kahlúa® or coffee liquor (optional)

tools

2 piping bags
Round piping tip (¼" [6 mm] in diameter) or piping tip of your choice

First, make the Coffee Macaron Shells by following the directions on page 35. Follow the instructions on page 148 of the Decorating Techniques chapter to make the two-toned shells. Dye half the batter with brown gel food coloring, and leave the other half undyed.

Line a piping bag with a piping tip to pipe the Caramel Coffee Buttercream onto the shells. Set aside.

To make the Salted Caramel Sauce, heat the sugar in a medium saucepan with a heavy bottom over medium heat, stirring constantly to help the sugar melt evenly. The sugar will begin to form a brown syrup as it slowly melts.

After about 3 minutes, the sugar granules should have melted and the syrup should be light brown. If the sugar has melted but the syrup is still white, cook for another 30 seconds or so until it becomes a light amber color. Once the sugar melts and the syrup has achieved the desired color, immediately lower the heat to low and add the cream. It's very important to avoid overcooking or burning the sugar. If the sugar cooks too much at this point, the caramel sauce will be hard once it cools down, or it will taste bitter.

Pour the cream over the amber-colored syrup. Be very careful as you pour, because the mixture will bubble up fiercely. Wear heat-resistant gloves or keep your hands away from the top of the pan to prevent burning yourself.

As soon as you add the heavy cream, some of the sugar will crystallize, and that's okay. Continue to stir for 30 seconds over medium-low heat while the sugar remelts.

(continued)

Once the sugar has remelted, add the butter and the salt, and stir the mixture for another 30 seconds.

As soon as you notice the butter has almost entirely melted in the caramel sauce, remove the pan from the heat. Continue to stir for another 20 seconds or so, until the butter melts entirely. It is very important not to overcook the sauce at any point, or it will become too hard as it cools down.

Pour the sauce into a heat-proof bowl, add the vanilla and stir. If there are bits of crystallized sugar in the sauce, pour the sauce through a strainer after you take it off the heat. Let the caramel sauce cool down completely before using it.

You will use some of the sauce for the Caramel Coffee Buttercream, and the rest will be used to fill the center of the macarons. The sauce has to be exactly at room temperature to be used in the buttercream and to fill the macarons. If the sauce is cold, it will be too hard to use, so don't store it in the fridge to cool it down. If the sauce is too warm, it will melt the butter in the frosting. If you make the sauce the day before and store it in the fridge, microwave it in a heat-safe bowl for 5-second intervals, stirring in between until the caramel is melted. Then, let it sit out until it comes to room temperature.

To make the Caramel Coffee Buttercream, begin by beating the butter with an electric mixer for about 1 minute until it begins to get creamy. Then, add the room-temperature caramel sauce to the bowl, along with the powdered sugar, espresso powder and Kahlúa (if using). Stir on low speed until the sugar has incorporated with the other ingredients, then increase the speed to medium and finish whipping for another 2 minutes. Transfer the buttercream to the prepared piping bag.

To assemble the macarons, pipe a ring of Caramel Coffee Buttercream around the edges of each bottom shell, then transfer the caramel sauce to a piping bag and snip the end with scissors. Pipe about ¼ teaspoon of caramel sauce in the center of each macaron, and then top with another shell.

Let the macarons chill, covered, in the fridge overnight before serving, then let them sit at room temperature for 10 to 20 minutes before enjoying.

The Caramel Macchiato Macarons will store well, covered, in the fridge for up to 5 days, or in the freezer, in an airtight container, for up to a month.

dalgona coffee macarons

Coffee lovers gather 'round! These Dalgona Coffee Macarons are not for the faint of heart—from top to bottom, it's coffee all the way. The creamy and fluffy Dalgona Cream Cheese Frosting is bold and has a bittersweet finish, balanced out by the sweetness of the espresso-flavored shells. It's a combination that will send you flying high!

yield: 20 (1½" [4-cm]) macaron sandwiches

1 batch Coffee Macaron Shells (page 35) dyed with a few drops of brown gel food coloring

dalgona cream cheese frosting

1 tbsp (6 g) instant coffee granules or espresso powder
1 tbsp (12 g) granulated sugar
1 tbsp (15 ml) water
4 tbsp (56 g) cream cheese, at room temperature
2 tbsp (28 g) unsalted butter, at room temperature
1½–2 cups (188–250 g) powdered sugar, sifted, plus more as needed

for decoration

⅓ cup (56 g) chocolate chips
3 tbsp (28 g) chocolate sprinkles
¼ cup (21 g) coffee beans

tools

2 piping bags
Large star piping tip (⅓" [1 cm] in diameter) or piping tip of your choice

First, make the Coffee Macaron Shells by following the directions on page 35, adding a few drops of brown gel food coloring when instructed.

Line a piping bag with a piping tip to pipe the Dalgona Cream Cheese Frosting onto the shells. Set aside.

To make the Dalgona Cream Cheese Frosting, combine the instant coffee, granulated sugar and water in a small bowl. With a hand mixer, whip the mixture on high speed for 4 to 6 minutes, until creamy and fluffy. It's best not to use a stand mixer when whipping the coffee mixture, because the whisk won't reach the bottom of the bowl. You can also whisk it by hand, but it will be quite the arm workout and take about 12 minutes of whipping.

Once the coffee mixture has been whipped to fluffy and sturdy peaks, set it aside.

In a separate bowl, beat the cream cheese and butter together with a mixer on medium-high speed for 2 minutes. Add the whipped coffee mixture and powdered sugar to the cream cheese mixture. Mix on low speed until combined, then raise the speed to medium-high and whip for another minute until fluffy and smooth. If the frosting is too runny, add more powdered sugar as needed, a couple of tablespoons (16 g) at a time, until you achieve the proper consistency.

Transfer the frosting to the prepared piping bag.

To decorate the top shells, place the chocolate in a small heat-proof bowl and microwave it for 15-second intervals, stirring in between, until completely melted. Transfer the chocolate to a piping bag, snip the end with scissors and drizzle chocolate over 20 of the shells. While the chocolate is still wet, top the shells with sprinkles and coffee beans.

To assemble the macarons, pipe the Dalgona Cream Cheese Frosting on the bottom shells, and top with a decorated shell.

Let the macarons chill, covered, in the fridge overnight before serving, then let them sit at room temperature for 10 to 20 minutes before enjoying.

The Dalgona Coffee Macarons will store well, covered, in the fridge for up to 5 days, or in the freezer, in an airtight container, for up to a month.

maple brown butter macarons

These Maple Brown Butter Macarons are exceptionally delicious and rich! The brown butter in the frosting adds nutty and deep notes that are enhanced by the robust maple syrup. The result is a sweet and bold flavor combination that will absolutely amaze everyone who tries it.

yield: 20 (1½" [4-cm]) macaron sandwiches

1 batch Plain Macaron Shells (page 24) dyed with a few drops of brown gel food coloring, if desired

maple brown butter frosting

4 tbsp (56 g) unsalted butter

2 cups (250 g) powdered sugar, sifted, plus more as needed

¼ cup (60 ml) maple syrup

1 tbsp (15 ml) heavy cream, plus more as needed

¼ tsp maple or vanilla extract

for decoration

2½ tbsp (28 g) caramel chips or candy melts

¼ cup (38 g) gold sprinkles (optional)

tools

2 piping bags

Round piping tip (½" [1.3 cm] in diameter) or piping tip of your choice

Line a piping bag with a piping tip to pipe the Maple Brown Butter Frosting onto the shells. Set aside.

To make the Maple Brown Butter Frosting, begin by heating the butter in a saucepan over medium heat, stirring occasionally, until the butter has melted.

Soon the butter will start to foam and sizzle, but continue to cook it, stirring often. The total cooking time for the butter should be 5 to 10 minutes. Once the butter turns golden, and you notice solid brown bits sinking to the bottom of the saucepan, it's time to remove it from the heat.

Pour the brown butter into a heat-proof bowl and let it sit until it cools down completely.

Add the cooled butter to the bowl of an electric mixer. Add the powdered sugar, and begin to mix on low. Add the maple syrup, and beat the mixture together on medium for 1 minute. If the frosting is too dry and thick, add the cream at this point. Note that if the consistency is already right without the cream, you may omit it. Continue to beat until completely smooth. If the frosting is too runny, add more powdered sugar as needed, 1 tablespoon (8 g) at a time, and if the frosting is too thick, add more cream to thin it out, 1 teaspoon at a time, until the proper consistency is achieved. Add the maple extract to the frosting and mix until incorporated. Transfer the frosting to the prepared piping bag.

To assemble the macarons, pipe the Maple Brown Butter Frosting on each bottom shell and then top with another shell.

To decorate the macarons, place the caramel chips in a small heat-proof bowl and microwave them for 15-second intervals, stirring in between, until completely melted. Transfer the melted caramel chips to a piping bag, snip the end with scissors and drizzle some over the macarons. While the caramel is still wet, add gold sprinkles if you'd like.

Let the macarons chill, covered, in the fridge overnight before serving, then let them sit at room temperature for 10 to 20 minutes before enjoying.

The Maple Brown Butter Macarons will store well, covered, in the fridge for up to 5 days, or in the freezer, in an airtight container, for up to a month.

tip: This frosting flavor also pairs wonderfully with Espresso Shells (page 35)! The slight bitterness of the espresso contrasts nicely with the sweet, bold Maple Brown Butter Frosting.

caramel s'mores macarons

How do we make s'mores even better? Add caramel to them! This delicious treat features chocolate macaron shells filled with a toasted Marshmallow Frosting and gooey Salted Caramel Sauce core. To really drive this incredible macaron home, the top of the shells are dipped in melted chocolate and decorated with more caramel sauce and graham cracker crumbs. Toasting the marshmallow adds another complex layer of flavor to this sweet and indulgent combo.

*See image on page 41.

yield: 20 (1½" [4-cm]) macaron sandwiches

1 batch Chocolate Macaron Shells (page 30)

salted caramel sauce
½ cup (100 g) granulated sugar
¼ cup (60 ml) heavy cream
2½ tbsp (35 g) unsalted butter
¼ tsp kosher salt
½ tsp vanilla extract

for decoration
½ cup (85 g) chopped chocolate
2½ tbsp (37 ml) Salted Caramel Sauce, at room temperature
⅓ cup (33 g) graham cracker crumbs

marshmallow frosting
2 egg whites (30 g)
½ cup (100 g) granulated sugar
¼ tsp cream of tartar
⅛ tsp fine sea salt
1 tsp vanilla extract

tools
2 piping bags
Round piping tip (¼" [6 mm] in diameter) or piping tip of your choice
Candy thermometer
Kitchen torch (optional)

First, make the Chocolate Macaron Shells by following the directions on page 30.

Line a piping bag with a piping tip to pipe the Marshmallow Frosting onto the shells. Set aside.

To make the Salted Caramel Sauce, heat the sugar in a medium saucepan with a heavy bottom over medium heat, stirring constantly to help the sugar melt evenly. The sugar will begin to form a brown syrup as it slowly melts.

After about 3 minutes, the sugar granules should have melted and the syrup should be light brown. If the sugar has melted but the syrup is still white, cook for another 30 seconds or so until it becomes a light amber color. Once the sugar melts and the syrup has achieved the desired color, immediately lower the heat to low and add the cream. It's very important to avoid overcooking or burning the sugar. If the sugar cooks too much at this point, the caramel sauce will be hard once it cools down, or it will taste bitter.

Pour the cream over the amber-colored syrup. Be very careful as you pour, because the mixture will bubble up fiercely. Wear heat-resistant gloves or keep your hands away from the top of the pan to prevent burning yourself.

As soon as you add the heavy cream, some of the sugar will crystallize, and that's okay. Continue to stir for 30 seconds over medium-low heat while the sugar remelts.

Once the sugar has remelted, add the butter and the salt, and stir the mixture for another 30 seconds.

As soon as you notice the butter has almost entirely melted in the caramel sauce, remove the pan from the heat. Continue to stir for another 20 seconds or so, until the butter melts entirely. It is very important not to overcook the sauce at any point, or it will become too hard as it cools down.

Pour the sauce into a heat-proof bowl, add the vanilla and stir. If there are bits of crystallized sugar in the sauce, pour the sauce through a strainer after you take it off the heat. Let the caramel sauce cool down completely before using it.

Now it's time to decorate the top shells. Place the chocolate in a small heat-proof bowl and microwave it for 15-second intervals, stirring in between, until completely melted.

Dip the top of 20 macaron shells in the melted chocolate, and then place each shell on a baking sheet. Place the baking sheet in the fridge so the chocolate will dry. It should take about 5 minutes. Then, place 2½ tablespoons (37 ml) of the room-temperature caramel sauce into a piping bag, snip the end with scissors and drizzle the caramel over the chocolate-dipped shells. Finish with a sprinkle of graham cracker crumbs on top.

To make the Marshmallow Frosting, combine the egg whites, sugar, cream of tartar and salt in a heat-proof bowl. Set the bowl over a pot of barely simmering water to form a double boiler. Make sure the bottom of the bowl isn't touching the water, to prevent the whites from cooking.

Whisk the mixture for a few minutes until it reaches 140°F (60°C) on a candy thermometer. Once the syrup is to temperature, remove the bowl from the double boiler. Whip the syrup with an electric mixer fitted with a whisk attachment for about 5 minutes on high speed. Add the vanilla and mix to combine. By this point, the meringue should have firm peaks and be fluffy and glossy. If not, continue to whip, as some mixers might take longer to get there. Transfer the frosting to the prepared piping bag. The Marshmallow Frosting has to be piped immediately after being made. It will hold up nicely after it is piped, but if you don't pipe it right away, it will begin to deflate and become runny.

To assemble the macarons, pipe a ring of Marshmallow Frosting around the edges of each bottom shell. Then, use a kitchen torch to toast the sides of the marshmallow frosting.

Spoon a bit of room-temperature Salted Caramel Sauce in the center of each macaron, and top with a decorated shell.

Let the macarons chill, covered, in the fridge overnight before serving, then let them sit at room temperature for 10 to 20 minutes before enjoying.

The Caramel S'mores Macarons will store well, covered, in the fridge for up to 5 days, or in the freezer, in an airtight container, for up to a month.

spiced and cozy

When it's time to get cozy and snug, it's also time to get baking! The macarons in this chapter are brimming with spices, nostalgic flavors and delicious combinations. The Bourbon Eggnog Custard Macarons (page 64) will make you want to go caroling in July, and you won't find a flavor you'll want to cuddle up with more than the Churros Macarons (page 79). The White Russian Macarons (page 73) will be the perfect treat for your best date night ever! There are plenty of scrumptious recipes in this chapter that will keep you tucked up in the kitchen, baking to your heart's content.

bourbon eggnog custard macarons

These Bourbon Eggnog Custard Macarons were made to be enjoyed by the fireplace, cozied up with a blanket, as you read a book or watch a show. They are filled with a Bourbon Eggnog Custard surrounded by a creamy Eggnog German Buttercream. The bourbon lends a gentle heat to the smooth custard filling, which is enhanced even further by the warming spices found all throughout each layer of the macarons. This is the type of flavor that will leave you feeling all fuzzy inside!

yield: 20 (1½" [4-cm]) macaron sandwiches

1 batch Spiced Macaron Shells (page 34) made with ½ tsp of the Spice Mix (recipe below) added in place of the spices. Sprinkle ¼ cup (38 g) of gold sprinkles and ½ tsp of additional Spice Mix on top of the shells before baking.

spice mix
½ tsp ground cinnamon
½ tsp ground nutmeg
½ tsp ground cloves

bourbon eggnog custard
¾ cup (180 ml) eggnog
2 tbsp (25 g) granulated sugar
1 tbsp (7.5 g) cornstarch
1 egg yolk
½ tsp bourbon
¼ tsp vanilla extract
¼ tsp Spice Mix

eggnog german buttercream
4 tbsp (56 g) unsalted butter, softened
¼ cup (70 g) Bourbon Eggnog Custard, chilled
1 cup (125 g) powdered sugar, sifted, plus more as needed
¼ tsp Spice Mix
½ tbsp (7 ml) milk or water, as needed

tools
Piping bag
Open star piping tip (¼" [6 mm] in diameter) or piping tip of your choice

First, prepare the Spice Mix by combining the ground cinnamon, nutmeg and cloves in a small bowl. Then, make the Spiced Macaron Shells by following the directions on page 34, using ½ teaspoon of the Spice Mix in place of the spices. Right after piping the shells, tapping the trays and poking the bubbles out, sprinkle the shells with ¼ cup (38 g) of gold sprinkles and ½ teaspoon of the Spice Mix before baking.

Line a piping bag with a piping tip to pipe the Eggnog German Buttercream onto the shells. Set aside.

To make the Bourbon Eggnog Custard, heat the eggnog in a small saucepan with a heavy bottom over medium heat for about 3 minutes, until it is almost boiling. While the eggnog heats, in a large bowl, whisk together the sugar, cornstarch and egg yolk. The mixture will seem very thick at first, but as you continue to whisk, it will become looser.

(continued)

Once the eggnog is almost boiling, remove the saucepan from the heat and pour a couple of tablespoons (30 ml) of the hot eggnog over the yolk and sugar mixture while whisking constantly. Gradually continue to add the remaining eggnog to the bowl as you whisk. This process is called tempering the eggs, which means slowly raising the temperature of the egg yolk to prevent it from cooking.

Once the hot eggnog has all been incorporated, pour the eggnog mixture back into the saucepan you first used to heat it, straining it through a fine-mesh sieve to catch any bits of yolk that may have cooked. Then, use a spatula or wooden spoon to stir the custard over medium-low heat. Don't stop stirring, because stopping will cause the custard to stick to the bottom of the pan. Keep cooking and stirring for 2 to 3 minutes, until it gets kind of lumpy, and then it will start to get smooth and thick.

When the whole mixture is creamy and smooth, turn the heat off. Immediately transfer the custard to a heat-proof bowl. Add the bourbon, vanilla and Spice Mix, stirring to combine. Cover the custard with a piece of plastic wrap placed directly on its surface and place the bowl in the fridge until it is completely cool.

To make the Eggnog German Buttercream, first make sure that the custard is cold. Remove the cold custard from the fridge, measure out ¼ cup (70 g) and set it aside. Beat the butter in a bowl with a mixer for 1 minute, until it starts to become creamy. It's very important that the butter isn't too soft when making the buttercream, or it will be too runny. Make sure the butter is between 68 and 72°F (20 and 22°C). Next add the cold ¼ cup (70 g) of custard to the butter and continue to beat with the mixer for another minute.

Add the powdered sugar and Spice Mix to the bowl, and mix on low speed until the sugar is incorporated with the other ingredients. Increase the speed to medium or medium-high, and continue to beat the buttercream for another minute, until creamy. If the buttercream is too runny, add more powdered sugar as needed, 1 tablespoon (8 g) at a time, and if the buttercream is too thick, add milk or water to thin it out, 1 teaspoon at a time, until the proper consistency is achieved. Transfer the buttercream to the prepared piping bag.

To assemble the macarons, pipe small dollops of Eggnog German Buttercream around the edges of each bottom shell. Then, spoon some of the Bourbon Eggnog Custard into the center. Top with another shell.

Let the macarons chill, covered, in the fridge overnight before serving, then let them sit at room temperature for 10 to 20 minutes before enjoying.

The Bourbon Eggnog Custard Macarons will store well, covered, in the fridge for up to 5 days, or in the freezer, in an airtight container, for up to a month.

note: If you don't like cloves, or if you'd like to substitute any of the spices, you can use allspice or even ground ginger instead. If you don't want to use either of those, increase the amounts of any of the other spices that you are using.

pink peppercorn pistachio macarons

How to elevate an already outstanding macaron flavor such as pistachio? I've got the secret ingredient for you: a dash of pink peppercorn! The pink peppercorn will add a nice touch of spunk and attitude to the mellow pistachio. A well-rounded pepper—not too peppery or pungent—pink peppercorns are very fruity and gently sweet. Their flavor is super delicate and fragrant, with floral notes that pair so well with the buttery pistachios. This is a flavor combination that you will cherish forever.

*See image on page 63.

yield: 20 (1½" [4-cm]) macaron sandwiches

1 batch Pistachio Macaron Shells (page 38) dyed with a few drops of green gel food coloring. Sprinkle 1 tsp of finely crushed pink peppercorn over the shells before baking.

pink peppercorn pistachio buttercream

6 tbsp (85 g) unsalted butter, at room temperature

2 cups (250 g) powdered sugar, sifted, plus more as needed

1/3 cup (28 g) finely ground pistachios

1 tbsp (15 ml) milk, plus more as needed

1/2 tsp vanilla extract

1/4 tsp finely crushed pink peppercorn, plus more to taste

tools

Piping bag

Large open star piping tip (1/3" [1 cm] in diameter) or piping tip of your choice

First, make the Pistachio Macaron Shells by following the directions on page 38, adding a few drops of green gel food coloring to the batter when instructed. Right after piping the shells, tapping the trays and poking the air bubbles out, sprinkle the shells with 1 teaspoon of finely crushed pink peppercorn before baking.

Line a piping bag with a piping tip to pipe the Pink Peppercorn Pistachio Buttercream onto the shells. Set aside.

To make the Pink Peppercorn Pistachio Buttercream, beat the butter in a large bowl with an electric mixer for about 2 minutes, until light and fluffy. With the mixer off, add the powdered sugar, pistachios and milk to the bowl. Be sure the pistachios are very finely ground, otherwise the buttercream might be lumpy and hard to pipe. Mix on low speed until all the ingredients are incorporated. Once you no longer see streaks of dry powdered sugar, beat the mixture on medium-high speed for 1 minute, until creamy and smooth.

If the buttercream is too runny, add more powdered sugar as needed, 1 tablespoon (8 g) at a time, and if the buttercream is too thick, add more milk to thin it out, 1 teaspoon at a time, until the proper consistency is achieved. Add the vanilla and finely crushed pink peppercorn and mix to combine. Taste the buttercream and add more pink peppercorn if desired. A little goes a long way, so it's best to add only 1/4 teaspoon at first. Transfer the buttercream to the prepared piping bag.

To assemble the macarons, pipe the Pink Peppercorn Pistachio Buttercream on each bottom shell, and top with another shell.

Let the macarons chill, covered, in the fridge overnight before serving, then let them sit at room temperature for 10 to 20 minutes before enjoying.

The Pink Peppercorn Pistachio Macarons will store well, covered, in the fridge for up to 5 days, or in the freezer, in an airtight container, for up to a month.

black sesame matcha macarons

Black sesame and matcha is a grown-up, sophisticated flavor combination that might pleasantly surprise your taste buds. The matcha shells are sweet, with a gentle herbal aftertaste, while the Black Sesame Buttercream filling is slightly bitter, very nutty and not overly sweet, which makes them an excellent match. I would pair these macarons with a smooth and creamy matcha latte to help bring out the bitter and nutty notes even more. The addition of almond extract to the filling is a must, though a little will go a very long way. It seals the deal by enhancing every layer of flavor without being too overpowering.

yield: 20 (1½" [4-cm]) macaron sandwiches

1 batch Matcha Macaron Shells (page 33). Sprinkle 3 tbsp (27 g) of black sesame seeds over the shells before baking.

black sesame buttercream

¼ cup (35 g) black sesame seeds

4 tbsp (56 g) unsalted butter, at room temperature

1½ cups (188 g) powdered sugar, sifted, plus more as needed

1 tbsp (15 ml) milk, plus more as needed

Dash of almond extract

tools

Piping bag

Round piping tip (½" [1.3 cm] in diameter) or piping tip of your choice

First, make the Matcha Macaron Shells by following the directions on page 33. Right after piping the shells, tapping the trays and popping the air bubbles, sprinkle 3 tablespoons (27 g) of black sesame seeds over the shells before baking.

Line a piping bag with a piping tip to pipe the Black Sesame Buttercream onto the shells. Set aside.

To make the Black Sesame Buttercream, process the black sesame seeds in a small food processor or spice grinder for 2 to 3 minutes, until they turn into a paste.

Next, whip the butter with an electric mixer at medium-high speed for 1 to 2 minutes, until fluffy. Add the black sesame seed paste, powdered sugar and milk to the bowl. Mix on low speed until the ingredients are incorporated together. Increase the speed to medium or medium-high, and whip the buttercream for another 2 minutes, until creamy and fluffy. If the buttercream is too runny, add more powdered sugar as needed, 1 tablespoon (8 g) at a time, and if the buttercream is too thick, add more milk to thin it out, 1 teaspoon at a time, until the proper consistency is achieved. Add the almond extract and mix until combined. Transfer the buttercream to the prepared piping bag.

To fill the macarons, pipe a dollop of Black Sesame Frosting on each bottom shell, and then top with another shell.

Let the macarons chill, covered, in the fridge overnight before serving, then let them sit at room temperature for 10 to 20 minutes before enjoying.

These Black Sesame Matcha Macarons will store well, covered, in the fridge for up to 5 days, or in the freezer, in an airtight container, for up to a month.

peppermint mocha macarons

These macarons feature Chocolate Espresso Shells filled with a fabulous dark chocolate ganache—a flavor profile that could only be enhanced by the addition of peppermint. The contrast of the deep mocha flavor and refreshing peppermint is a treat for the senses.

yield: 20 (1½" [4-cm]) macaron sandwiches

1 batch Chocolate Macaron Shells (page 30) made with ¼ tsp espresso powder added to the dry ingredients

peppermint dark chocolate ganache

13½ tbsp (150 g) chopped dark chocolate or chocolate chips

7 tbsp (105 ml) heavy cream

½ tsp peppermint extract

for decoration

2½ tbsp (28 g) chopped dark chocolate or chocolate chips

3 tbsp (30 g) crushed candy canes

tools

2 piping bags

Round piping tip (½" [1.3 cm] in diameter) or piping tip of your choice

First, make the Chocolate Macaron Shells, following the directions on page 30 and adding ¼ teaspoon of espresso powder to the dry ingredients.

Line a piping bag with a piping tip to pipe the Peppermint Dark Chocolate Ganache onto the shells. Set aside.

To make the Peppermint Dark Chocolate Ganache, begin by placing the chocolate in a heat-proof bowl. Set it aside.

Heat the cream in a small saucepan over medium heat, or in a small bowl in the microwave, until it almost comes to a boil. This should take a couple of minutes in the saucepan and about 30 seconds in the microwave Then, pour the hot cream over the chocolate. Cover the bowl with a plate or towel and let it sit for 1 minute, then stir with a spatula until the chocolate has melted entirely. Once the chocolate has melted and the ganache is smooth, add the peppermint extract and mix to combine.

Set the ganache aside to cool to room temperature. You can place it in the fridge for about 30 minutes, or until thick, stirring every so often. If the ganache gets too hard, microwave it for 3- to 5-second intervals, stirring in between to obtain a smooth, spreadable consistency. When the ganache is at room temperature, thick and spreadable, transfer it to the prepared piping bag.

To decorate the top shells, place the chocolate in a small heat-proof bowl and microwave it for 15-second intervals, stirring in between, until completely melted. Transfer the melted chocolate to a piping bag, snip the end with scissors and drizzle some chocolate over 20 of the shells. While the chocolate is still wet, sprinkle crushed candy canes on top of the shells.

To assemble the macarons, pipe a bit of ganache on each bottom shell, then top with a decorated shell.

Let the macarons chill, covered, in the fridge overnight before serving, then let them sit at room temperature for 10 to 20 minutes before enjoying.

The Peppermint Mocha Macarons will store well, covered, in the fridge for up to 5 days, or in the freezer, in an airtight container, for up to a month.

white russian macarons

Here we have a sweet and creamy buttercream laced with vodka and coffee liquor, sandwiched between espresso-flavored macaron shells—a high-spirited flavor profile that packs a punch. These White Russian Macarons are spunky yet dainty and would make the perfect nightcap.

yield: 20 (1½" [4-cm]) macaron sandwiches

1 batch Coffee Macaron Shells (page 35)

white russian buttercream

6 tbsp (85 g) unsalted butter, at room temperature

2½ cups (312 g) powdered sugar, sifted, plus more as needed

2 tbsp (30 ml) good quality vodka

1 tbsp (15 ml) Kahlúa or coffee liquor

1 tbsp (15 ml) heavy cream, plus more as needed

for decoration

3 tbsp (30 g) white chocolate, chopped

¼ cup (38 g) white crispearls

tools

2 piping bags

Large star piping tip (⅓" [1 cm] in diameter) or piping tip of your choice

First, make the Coffee Macaron Shells by following the directions on page 35.

Line a piping bag with a piping tip to pipe the White Russian Buttercream onto the shells. Set aside.

To make the White Russian Buttercream, beat the butter in a large bowl with a mixer on medium-high speed for 2 minutes until fluffy. Add the powdered sugar, vodka, Kahlúa and cream to the bowl, and mix on low speed until the ingredients are incorporated. Once you no longer see streaks of dry powdered sugar, beat the mixture on medium-high speed for 1 to 2 minutes, until creamy and fluffy. If the buttercream is too runny, add more powdered sugar as needed, 1 tablespoon (8 g) at a time, and if the buttercream is too thick, add more cream to thin it out, 1 teaspoon at a time, until the proper consistency is achieved. Transfer the buttercream to the prepared piping bag.

To decorate the top shells, place the chocolate in a small heat-proof bowl and microwave it for 15-second intervals, stirring in between, until completely melted. Transfer the chocolate to a piping bag, snip the end with scissors and drizzle melted chocolate over 20 of the macaron shells. While the chocolate is still wet, place crispearls on the shells.

To assemble the macarons, pipe the White Russian Buttercream on each bottom shell and then top with a decorated shell.

Let the macarons chill, covered, in the fridge overnight before serving, then let them sit at room temperature for 10 to 20 minutes before enjoying.

The White Russian Macarons will store well, covered, in the fridge for up to 5 days, or in the freezer, in an airtight container, for up to a month.

sugar plum macarons

Sugar plums immediately make me think of the holiday season, thanks to the warm spices and bold flavors that are nostalgic and mesmerizing to the palate. Sugar plum is a mixture of nuts, dried fruits and spices that would normally be rolled into truffles and dredged in sparkling sugar, but here, the mixture is used to fill the center of the macarons, surrounded by a ring of Honey Cardamom Buttercream. The flavors are sophisticated and very grown-up, and I can imagine myself snacking on these macarons on a cold night while watching a snowfall.

yield: 20 (1½" [4-cm]) macaron sandwiches

1 batch Plain Macaron Shells (page 24) dyed with a few drops of purple gel food coloring. Sprinkle 3 tbsp (37 g) of purple crystal sugar over the shells before baking.

sugar plum mixture

1½ tbsp (14 g) slivered almonds
1½ tbsp (14 g) dried cherries
1½ tbsp (14 g) dried cranberries
2 prunes (14 g)
2 dried apricots (14 g)
2 tbsp (8 g) powdered sugar, sifted
1 tsp honey
Pinch of ground fennel
Pinch of ground cardamom
Pinch of ground caraway seeds

honey cardamom buttercream

4 tbsp (56 g) unsalted butter, at room temperature
2 tbsp (30 ml) honey
1½ cups (188 g) powdered sugar, sifted
¼ tsp ground cardamom
½ tsp vanilla extract

tools
Piping bag
Closed star piping tip (½" [1.3 cm] in diameter) or piping tip of your choice

First, make the Plain Macaron Shells by following the directions on page 24, adding a few drops of purple gel food coloring to the batter when instructed. Right after piping the shells, tapping the trays and poking the air bubbles out, sprinkle 3 tablespoons (37 g) of purple crystal sugar over the shells before baking.

Line a piping bag with a piping tip to pipe the Honey Cardamom Buttercream onto the shells. Set aside.

To make the Sugar Plum Mixture, add the almonds, cherries, cranberries, prunes, apricots, powdered sugar, honey, fennel, cardamom and caraway seeds to a blender or small food processor. Process the ingredients for 3 to 7 minutes, depending on how powerful your blender is, until a paste has formed. Set the mixture aside.

To make the Honey Cardamom Buttercream, beat the butter in a large bowl with a mixer on medium speed for 1 minute. Add the honey, powdered sugar, cardamom and vanilla to the bowl, and mix on low speed until the ingredients are incorporated. Increase the speed to medium, and continue to beat for about 1 minute, until fluffy. Transfer the buttercream to the prepared piping bag.

To assemble the macarons, pipe a ring of frosting around each bottom shell, then spoon some of the Sugar Plum mixture in the middle. Top the macarons with another shell.

Let the macarons chill, covered, in the fridge overnight before serving, then let them sit at room temperature for 10 to 20 minutes before enjoying.

The Sugar Plum Macarons will store well, covered, in the fridge for up to 5 days, or in the freezer, in an airtight container, for up to a month.

chai oatmeal latte macarons

I've always wanted to incorporate oatmeal into a macaron flavor, so I tried to make a custard with oats. It came out alright, but something was missing: I needed something to complement the flavor and give it some oomph. So I went with one of my favorite spice blends: chai! Here, chai-spiced macaron shells are filled with a Chai Oatmeal Custard and a Chai Swiss Meringue Buttercream. There's a nice contrast between the delicate and airy frosting and the hearty oatmeal filling. The milk in the oatmeal custard is also infused with chai tea, which makes it all the more flavorful.

yield: 20 (1½" [4-cm]) macaron sandwiches

1 batch Spiced Macaron Shells (page 34) made with ¼ tsp chai spice added in place of the spices and dyed with a few drops of blue gel food coloring.

chai oatmeal custard

¾ cup (180 ml) milk
2 chai tea bags
2 tbsp (25 g) granulated sugar
1 tbsp (8 g) cornstarch
1 large egg yolk
2 tbsp (11 g) quick cooking oats
½ tsp vanilla extract
¼ tsp chai spice

chai swiss meringue buttercream

10 tbsp (141 g) unsalted butter, softened
2 egg whites (30 g)
½ cup (100 g) granulated sugar
½ tsp vanilla extract
¼ tsp chai spice (or more to taste)

for decoration

⅓ cup (56 g) chopped white chocolate
3 tbsp (17 g) quick cooking oats

tools

2 piping bags
Round piping tip (¼" [6 mm] in diameter) or piping tip of your choice
Candy thermometer

First, make the Spiced Macaron Shells, following the directions on page 34 and adding the chai spice in place of the spices and a few drops of blue gel food coloring to the batter when instructed.

Line a piping bag with a piping tip to pipe the Chai Swiss Meringue Buttercream onto the shells. Set aside.

To make the Chai Oatmeal Custard, heat the milk and two chai tea bags in a small pot with a heavy bottom over medium heat. Bring the milk to a boil. Once the milk is boiling, turn off the heat and let the tea bags steep for 5 minutes. Meanwhile, in a separate bowl, whisk together the sugar, cornstarch and egg yolk. The mixture will seem very thick at first, but as you continue to whisk, it will become looser.

Discard the chai tea bags and reheat the milk briefly just so it's hot again. Pour a couple of tablespoons (30 ml) of the hot chai milk over the yolk and sugar mixture while whisking constantly. Gradually continue to add the remaining chai milk to the bowl as you whisk. This process is called tempering the eggs, which means slowly raising the temperature of the egg yolk to prevent it from cooking.

Once the chai milk has all been incorporated, pour the chai milk mixture back into the saucepan you first used to heat it, straining it through a fine-mesh sieve to catch any bits of yolk that may have cooked.

(continued)

Add the oats to the pan, and use a spatula or wooden spoon to stir the custard over medium-low heat. Don't stop stirring, or else the custard will stick to the bottom of the pan. Keep cooking and stirring for 2 to 3 minutes until it gets kind of lumpy, and then it will start to get smooth and thick.

When the whole mixture is creamy and smooth, turn the heat off. Immediately transfer the custard to a heat-proof bowl. Add the vanilla and the chai spice, stirring to combine. Cover the custard with a piece of plastic wrap placed directly on its surface and place the bowl in the fridge until it is completely cool.

To make the Chai Swiss Meringue Buttercream, remove the butter from the fridge 1 to 2 hours in advance. The butter needs to be softened, but not too soft, though it also shouldn't be cold. If the butter is too soft, the buttercream won't come together and will be too runny. If the butter is too cold, it will form lumps in the buttercream that won't incorporate with the frosting, and then you will be biting into chunks of butter when you eat it. The butter should be at around 68 to 72°F (20 to 22°C).

Place the egg whites and sugar in a heat-proof bowl. Set the bowl over a pot of barely simmering water to form a double boiler. Make sure the bottom of the bowl isn't touching the water, to prevent the whites from cooking. Whisk the mixture for about 5 minutes, until it reaches 140°F (60°C) on a candy thermometer. Basically, you are looking to melt the sugar granules, and also make the egg whites safe for consumption.

Once the syrup is to temperature, remove the bowl from the double boiler, and begin to whip it with an electric mixer on low speed. Gradually increase the speed to medium-high, and continue to whip until stiff peaks form. This usually takes 5 to 10 minutes because the meringue has to cool down to start forming the peaks, but depending on your mixer, it can even take up to 15 minutes. On speed 8 of my KitchenAid, it takes about 5 minutes for the meringue to form stiff peaks, but with my hand mixer, it can take 10 minutes or more.

Make sure the meringue achieves stiff peaks. If the peaks are not stiff enough before you start to add the butter, the frosting won't come together.

Cut the butter into very small pats, and once the meringue has reached stiff peaks, begin to add one pat of butter at a time, whisking it completely into the meringue before adding the next slab of butter. This whole process could take up to 15 minutes.

Once you are done adding the butter, the buttercream should already be firming up and becoming thick and creamy. If at this point the buttercream isn't doing any of those things, it's either because the butter was too soft or the meringue wasn't whipped enough. One way to troubleshoot it is to place the bowl in the fridge for about 10 minutes, and then try to whip it again.

Once all of the butter has been incorporated, and the buttercream is thick and fluffy, add the vanilla and the chai spices to the bowl. Whisk until completely incorporated. Transfer the buttercream to the prepared piping bag.

To decorate the top shells, place the chocolate in a small heat-proof bowl and microwave it for 15-second intervals, stirring in between, until completely melted. Place the chocolate in a piping bag and snip the end with scissors. Then, drizzle the chocolate over the macaron shells and top with oats.

To assemble the macarons, pipe a ring of Chai Swiss Meringue Buttercream around the edges of each bottom shell. Fill the center with about a ¼ teaspoon of the Chai Oatmeal Custard. Top with a decorated shell.

Let the macarons chill, covered, in the fridge overnight before serving, then let them sit at room temperature for 10 to 20 minutes before enjoying.

The Chai Oatmeal Latte Macarons will store well, covered, in the fridge for up to 5 days, or in the freezer, in an airtight container, for up to a month.

churros macarons

In this recipe, one of my favorite desserts takes macaron form. The shells are sprinkled with a sugar and cinnamon mixture before baking, which will give them a slightly crunchy texture that is quite delightful to bite into. The macarons are then filled with dulce de leche surrounded by Dulce de Leche Swiss Meringue Buttercream. If you can find a brand of dulce de leche that is thick enough and that holds its shape, you can pipe it directly onto the macarons and omit the buttercream. However, many brands are quite runny and may not hold up on their own. Regardless, dulce de leche is rich in flavor and has a sticky, fudgy texture that is exceptionally delicious.

yield: 20 (1½" [4-cm]) macaron sandwiches

1 batch Plain Macaron Shells (page 24). Sprinkle the shells with the Cinnamon Sugar Mix (recipe below) before baking.

cinnamon sugar mix

1 tbsp (12 g) granulated sugar
2 tsp (5 g) cinnamon

dulce de leche swiss meringue buttercream (see note)

10 tbsp (141 g) unsalted butter, softened
2 egg whites (30 g)
½ cup (100 g) granulated sugar
¼ cup (75 g) dulce de leche
½ tsp vanilla extract

for the filling

¼ cup (75 g) dulce de leche

tools

2 piping bags
Open star piping tip (¼" [6 mm] in diameter) or piping tip of your choice
Candy thermometer

First, prepare the Cinnamon Sugar Mix by combining the sugar and cinnamon in a small bowl. Then, make the Plain Macaron Shells, following the directions on page 24. Right after piping the shells, tapping the trays and poking the air bubbles out, sprinkle the Cinnamon Sugar Mix on top of the shells before baking. Be careful not to weigh down the macarons with too much of the mixture.

Line a piping bag with a piping tip to pipe the Dulce de Leche Swiss Meringue Buttercream onto the shells. Set aside.

To make the Dulce de Leche Swiss Meringue Buttercream, remove the butter from the fridge 1 to 2 hours in advance. The butter needs to be softened, but not too soft, though it also shouldn't be cold. If the butter is too soft, the buttercream won't come together and will be too runny. If the butter is too cold, it will form lumps in the buttercream that won't incorporate with the frosting, and then you will be biting into chunks of butter when you eat it. The butter should be at around 68 to 72°F (20 to 22°C).

Place the egg whites and sugar in a heat-proof bowl. Set the bowl over a pot of barely simmering water to form a double boiler. Make sure the bottom of the bowl isn't touching the water, to prevent the whites from cooking. Whisk the mixture for about 5 minutes, until it reaches 140°F (60°C) on a candy thermometer. Basically you are looking to melt the sugar granules, and also make the egg whites safe for consumption.

(continued)

Once the syrup is to temperature, remove the bowl from the double boiler, and begin to whip it with an electric mixer on low speed. Gradually increase the speed to medium-high, and continue to whip until stiff peaks form. This usually takes 5 to 10 minutes because the meringue has to cool down to start forming the peaks, but depending on your mixer, it can even take up to 15 minutes. On speed 8 of my KitchenAid, it takes about 5 minutes for the meringue to form stiff peaks, but with my hand mixer, it can take 10 minutes or more.

Make sure the meringue achieves stiff peaks. If the peaks are not stiff enough before you start to add the butter, the frosting won't come together.

Cut the butter into very small pats, and once the meringue has reached stiff peaks, begin to add one pat of butter at a time, whisking it completely into the meringue before adding the next slab of butter. This whole process could take up to 15 minutes.

Once you are done adding the butter, the buttercream should already be firming up and becoming thick and creamy. If at this point the buttercream isn't doing any of those things, it's either because the butter was too soft or the meringue wasn't whipped enough. One way to troubleshoot it is to place the bowl in the fridge for about 10 minutes, and then try to whip it again.

Once all of the butter has been incorporated, and the buttercream is thick and fluffy, add the dulce de leche and vanilla to the bowl. Whisk until completely incorporated. Place the buttercream in the prepared piping bag.

To assemble the macarons, pipe a ring of Dulce de Leche Swiss Meringue Buttercream around the edges of each bottom shell, then fill the center with dulce de leche. I like to put the dulce de leche in a piping bag and snip the end with scissors to make this task easier and less messy. Top with another shell.

Let the macarons chill, covered, in the fridge overnight before serving, then let them sit at room temperature for 10 to 20 minutes before enjoying.

The Churros Macarons will store well, covered, in the fridge for up to 5 days, or in the freezer, in an airtight container, for up to a month.

note: If you want to skip making the frosting and just use dulce de leche to fill the macarons instead, that is entirely possible. Find a brand of dulce de leche that is very thick so the dulce de leche is sturdy enough to not ooze all over the place. A good tip is to look for repostero dulce de leche, which you should be able to find online or in Latin food stores.

fresh
and fruity

Satisfy your sweet tooth with macarons that feature fresh and fruity flavors, perfect to kick back and relax with. The Piña Colada Macarons (page 87) will make you feel like you're sitting by the poolside, and there's truly nothing better than some Strawberry Shortcake Macarons (page 91), loaded with fresh strawberry flavor, to enjoy after a day of fun OR work. This chapter includes many other seasonal flavors and combinations that will totally make each day feel like a celebration!

matcha blueberry macarons

I can't think of a more perfect filling for Matcha Macaron Shells (page 33) than the combination of a sweet and smooth Matcha White Chocolate Ganache and an unbelievably tangy Blueberry Curd. Matcha and white chocolate were simply made for each other, and the only thing that could make the fusion even more enticing is the addition of a bright and lively fruit.

yield: 20 (1¹/₂" [4-cm]) macaron sandwiches

1 batch Matcha Macaron Shells (page 33), or a half batch of Matcha Macaron Shells and a half batch of Plain Macaron Shells (page 24) dyed with a few drops of purple gel food coloring

blueberry curd
¹/₂ cup (75 g) blueberries
2 tbsp (30 ml) lemon juice
1 large egg yolk
2 tbsp (25 g) granulated sugar
1 tbsp (14 g) unsalted butter, softened

matcha white chocolate ganache
1 cup (170 g) chopped white chocolate (see Note)
¹/₃ cup (78 ml) heavy cream, divided
³/₄ tsp matcha powder

tools
Piping bag
Round piping tip (¹/₄" [6 mm] in diameter) or piping tip of your choice
Candy thermometer

First, make either a full or half batch of Matcha Macaron Shells by following the directions on page 33. If making a half batch, also make a half batch of Plain Macaron Shells by following the directions on page 24 and adding a few drops of purple gel food coloring to the batter when instructed.

Line a piping bag with a piping tip to pipe the Matcha White Chocolate Ganache onto the shells. Set aside.

To make the Blueberry Curd, bring the blueberries and lemon juice to a boil in a small saucepan over medium heat and simmer for 5 minutes, stirring constantly and using the back of a spatula to pop the blueberries as they soften. Remove the pan from the heat, and transfer the mixture to a bowl, straining it through a sieve. Press down to extract as much liquid as possible. Discard the blueberry skins.

Meanwhile, whisk the yolk and sugar together in a bowl. Add the butter and continue to whisk until smooth. Slowly pour the blueberry juice into the bowl, whisking constantly. Once everything is incorporated, pour the mixture into a small saucepan. Slowly heat the mixture over medium-low heat, stirring constantly. Don't turn up the heat too high, or the egg will scramble.

Continue to cook over medium-low heat until the curd is thick enough to coat the back of a spoon. Use a candy thermometer to continually take the temperature of the curd. Remove the pan from the heat once it reaches 170°F (76°C). Transfer the curd to a bowl, and place it in the fridge to chill for 1 hour before using.

To make the Matcha White Chocolate Ganache, begin by placing the chocolate in a glass or stainless steel bowl. Set it aside.

(continued)

matcha blueberry macarons (continued)

In a separate bowl, combine 1 tablespoon (15 ml) of cream and the matcha powder, mixing with a spoon or fork until a paste is formed. Slowly add the rest of the cream, stirring constantly to prevent any lumps from forming.

Bring the matcha mixture to a boil in a small pan over medium heat, stirring occasionally to incorporate the ingredients. As soon as you see the first few bubbles, turn off the heat.

Pour the hot cream and matcha mixture over the chocolate, then cover the bowl with a towel and let it sit for 1 minute. Use a whisk to gently incorporate the chocolate and cream mixture. Continue to whisk gently until the chocolate has completely melted. If you notice lumps of chocolate in the ganache, you can strain them out, or heat the bowl in the microwave for 5-second intervals, stirring in between to ensure all the bits of chocolate have melted. However, be careful to avoid overheating the chocolate so it doesn't become lumpy and thick.

Set the ganache aside to cool to room temperature. It will thicken as it cools down. Once the Matcha White Chocolate Ganache is at room temperature, it should be thick, creamy and spreadable. Transfer it to the prepared piping bag.

To assemble the macarons, pipe a ring of Matcha White Chocolate Ganache around the edges of the bottom shells. Spoon some of the Blueberry Curd in the middle of each macaron, and top with another shell.

Let the macarons chill, covered, in the fridge overnight before serving, then let them sit at room temperature for 10 to 20 minutes before enjoying.

The Matcha Blueberry Macarons will store well, covered, in the fridge for up to 5 days, or in the freezer, in an airtight container, for up to a month.

note: Be sure to use real white chocolate made with at least 20 percent cocoa butter. If the ganache separates or curdles, add a tablespoon (15 ml) of cream to it, place it over a double boiler and gently stir until it comes back together. It might need another tablespoon (15 ml) of cream to do so. Continue to gently stir the ganache until it becomes slightly warm, then let it cool down again before using.

piña colada macarons

These Piña Colada Macarons are a perfect tropical blend of sweet coconut and tangy pineapple. The shells are coconut flavored, filled with a nutty and creamy Coconut Buttercream spiked with white rum and a delicious Pineapple Curd that you could just eat with a spoon right out of the bowl!

yield: 20 (1½" [4-cm]) macaron sandwiches

1 batch Coconut Macaron Shells (page 31)

pineapple curd
½ cup (120 ml) pineapple juice (see Note)
2 tbsp (28 g) unsalted butter
¼ cup (50 g) granulated sugar
2 large egg yolks
1 tbsp (15 ml) lemon juice

coconut buttercream
6 tbsp (85 g) unsalted butter, at room temperature
2 cups (250 g) powdered sugar, sifted, plus more as needed
2 tbsp (30 ml) coconut milk or coconut cream, plus more as needed
1 tsp white rum (optional)
¼ tsp coconut extract (optional)

for decoration
20 maraschino cherries

tools
2 piping bags
Round piping tip (¼" [6 mm] in diameter) or piping tip of your choice
Small open star piping tip
Candy thermometer

First, make the Coconut Macaron Shells, following the directions on page 31.

Line a piping bag with a piping tip to pipe the Coconut Buttercream onto the bottom shells. Line another piping bag with the small open star piping tip to pipe the Coconut Buttercream onto the top shells. Set aside.

To make the Pineapple Curd, bring the pineapple juice to a boil in a small saucepan over medium heat. Let the juice simmer for 10 to 20 minutes, until it has reduced to ¼ cup (60 ml). This will help concentrate the flavor of the pineapple and make it shine in the curd. Once the juice has reduced by half, set it aside and let it cool down for about 20 minutes.

Meanwhile, beat the butter and the sugar with an electric mixer for 30 seconds until incorporated. Add the yolks and mix until combined. Next, add the lemon juice and cooled pineapple juice and mix briefly.

Transfer the mixture to a small saucepan with a heavy bottom, and heat it over low heat, stirring constantly. Don't let the mixture come to a boil. Keep the heat very low, and don't stop stirring.

Continue cooking for 5 to 10 minutes, until the curd is thick enough to coat the back of a spoon. Use a candy thermometer to continually take the temperature of the curd. Remove the pan from the heat once it reaches 170°F (76°C). Transfer the curd to a bowl, straining it to remove any bits of cooked egg. Place the curd in the fridge to chill for 1 hour before using.

(continued)

To make the Coconut Buttercream, beat the butter in a large bowl with a mixer on medium-high speed for 2 minutes until light and fluffy. With the mixer off, add the powdered sugar and coconut milk to the bowl, and mix on low speed until the ingredients are incorporated. Once you no longer see streaks of dry powdered sugar, beat the mixture on medium-high speed for 1 minute, until creamy and smooth.

If the buttercream is too runny, add more powdered sugar as needed, 1 tablespoon (8 g) at a time, and if the buttercream is too thick, add more coconut milk to thin it out, 1 teaspoon at a time, until the proper consistency is achieved. Add the rum and coconut extract (if using), and mix to combine. You could always replace them with 1 teaspoon of vanilla instead. Transfer most of the buttercream to the prepared piping bag fitted with the round piping tip. Transfer the small remaining portion of buttercream to the other prepared piping bag fitted with the small open star piping tip.

To assemble the macarons, pipe a ring of the Coconut Buttercream around the edges of each bottom shell using the round piping tip. Then, spoon some of the Pineapple Curd in the center of each macaron, and top with another shell.

To decorate the macarons, pipe a bit of Coconut Buttercream onto the tops of the macarons using the small open star piping tip, then place a maraschino cherry on top.

Let the macarons chill, covered, in the fridge overnight before serving, then let them sit at room temperature for 10 to 20 minutes before enjoying.

The Piña Colada Macarons will store well, covered, in the fridge for up to 5 days, or in the freezer, in an airtight container, for up to a month.

note: Canned pineapple juice will work better for this recipe than fresh because it's often more concentrated.

strawberry shortcake macarons

Strawberry shortcake is a winning flavor. These macarons are a labor of love, as they feature a light and not overly sweet Mascarpone Filling, with Strawberry Jam in the center. The macaron sandwiches then get dipped in melted white chocolate and sprinkled with a Strawberry Biscuit Crumble. A few options are available to make this recipe a bit faster: You can use store-bought jam, and you could also roll the sides of the macarons in the biscuit crumble instead of doing the white chocolate dip. That being said, the best part of these Strawberry Shortcake Macarons is for sure the crumble, so don't skimp on it.

yield: 20 (1½" [4-cm]) macaron sandwiches

1 batch Freeze-Dried Fruit Shells (page 36) using freeze-dried strawberry powder and dyed with a few drops of pink gel food coloring.

strawberry jam
1 cup (150 g) chopped strawberries
3 tbsp (36 g) granulated sugar
1 tbsp (15 ml) lemon juice
2 tsp (5 g) cornstarch
1 tbsp (15 ml) cold water

strawberry biscuit crumble
3 tbsp (23 g) all-purpose flour
1 tbsp (12 g) granulated sugar
1½ tbsp (21 g) unsalted butter, at room temperature
1 tbsp (6 g) freeze-dried strawberries

mascarpone filling (see note)
¼ cup (60 ml) heavy whipping cream, cold
¾ cup (170 g) mascarpone cheese, cold
1–1½ cups (125–188 g) powdered sugar, sifted
¼ tsp vanilla extract

for decoration
½ cup (85 g) chopped white chocolate

tools
Piping bag
Round piping tip (¼" [6 mm] in diameter) or piping tip of your choice

First, make the Freeze-Dried Fruit Shells by following the directions on page 36, adding freeze-dried strawberry powder to the dry ingredients and pink gel food coloring to the batter when instructed.

Line a piping bag with a piping tip to pipe the Mascarpone Filling onto the shells. Set aside.

Next, make the Strawberry Jam. In a small saucepan, bring the strawberries, sugar and lemon juice to a boil and let it simmer over medium heat for 15 to 20 minutes, until the strawberries are falling apart. Use the back of a spoon to help mash the strawberries. If the mixture starts to dry out or stick to the pan, lower the heat and add a tablespoon (15 ml) of water to the pan.

In a small bowl, combine the cornstarch and cold water. Once the strawberries are soft and have fallen apart, add the cornstarch mixture to the pan and bring it to a simmer, stirring constantly for 1 or 2 minutes until the jam is very thick.

(continued)

Remove the pan from the heat and pour the jam into a bowl. Let it cool down, then cover it and place it in the fridge for about 2 hours until completely chilled.

To make the Strawberry Biscuit Crumble, preheat the oven to 325°F (160°C). In a small bowl, combine the flour, sugar and butter. Use a fork or a spatula to mix the ingredients together until a crumbly dough forms.

Spread the crumbly dough on top of a baking sheet lined with parchment paper or a silicone mat, and bake for 5 minutes. Remove the baking sheet from the oven, and stir the mixture with a spatula to separate it and create the crumbs. This also helps it all bake evenly.

Return the crumble back to the oven, and continue to bake for another 5 minutes. After that, give it another stir and determine if it needs to be baked another 4 to 5 minutes. The crumble should be slightly golden.

Remove the crumble from the oven and stir the freeze-dried strawberries into it. Let it cool down completely before using.

To make the Mascarpone Filling, be sure the cream is super cold and the mascarpone cheese isn't very liquid. Some brands of mascarpone cheese can be very runny, and you will need to drain it in a cheese cloth–lined strainer for a few hours in the fridge before using, or else the filling won't become stiff enough to pipe.

In a large bowl, whip the cream with an electric mixer at medium-high speed for 2 to 3 minutes, until stiff peaks form. Don't overwhip the cream, or it will separate and curdle. The peaks should be firm, but the cream shouldn't become chunky.

Once the cream is whipped, add the cold mascarpone cheese, 1 cup (125 g) of powdered sugar and the vanilla to the bowl. Mix on medium speed for another 1 to 2 minutes, until the ingredients are incorporated.

If the filling is too thin and soft, add the remaining powdered sugar and mix until incorporated. Transfer the filling to the prepared piping bag.

To assemble the macarons, pipe a ring of Mascarpone Filling around the edges of the bottom shells. Then, spoon some of the cooled Strawberry Jam in the middle, and top with another shell. Place the macarons in the fridge for about 1 hour to chill.

To decorate the macarons, place the chocolate in a small heat-proof bowl and microwave it for 15-second intervals, stirring in between, until completely melted. Remove the cold macarons from the fridge and dip half of each macaron in the melted chocolate, one by one. Let the excess chocolate drip off, then place the macarons on a baking sheet lined with silicone. While the chocolate is still wet, sprinkle the macarons with the Strawberry Biscuit Crumble.

Let the macarons chill, covered, in the fridge overnight before serving, then let them sit at room temperature for 10 to 20 minutes before enjoying.

The Strawberry Shortcake Macarons will store well, covered, in the fridge for up to 5 days, or in the freezer, in an airtight container, for up to a month.

note: The Mascarpone Filling shouldn't be made in advance, as it has to be piped immediately after being made. It will hold up fine after it is piped, but it will start to deflate and won't pipe well if it sits in the bowl or in the piping bag.

grape macarons

This is an uncomplicated yet remarkable macaron flavor. It's not every day that you see Grape Macarons at stores and bakeries. I recommend using a dark variety of grapes such as Concord to make the filling, because they tend to have a sweet, bold flavor. The Grape Jam is fairly easy to make, but you could always go the store-bought route. We are pairing it with a simple Vanilla Buttercream that lets the jam shine while still providing a much-desired creaminess to the macarons.

*See photo on page 83.

yield: 20 (1½" [4-cm]) macaron sandwiches

1 batch Plain Macaron Shells (page 24) made using the Multicolored Shells technique for two-tone shells demonstrated on page 148. Dye half the batter with a few drops of purple gel food coloring, and dye the other half with double the amount of purple gel food coloring.

grape jam

1 cup (142 g) dark grapes (such as Concord)
1 tbsp (12 g) granulated sugar
1 tbsp (15 ml) lemon juice
1½ tsp (4 g) cornstarch
1 tbsp (15 ml) cold water

vanilla buttercream

6 tbsp (85 g) unsalted butter, at room temperature
1½ cups (188 g) powdered sugar, sifted, plus more as needed
1 tbsp (15 ml) heavy cream, plus more as needed
1 tsp vanilla extract

tools

Piping bag
Round piping tip (¼" [6 mm] in diameter) or piping tip of your choice

First, make the Plain Macaron Shells by following the directions on page 24. Follow the instructions on page 148 of the Decorating Techniques chapter to make the two-toned shells. Dye half the batter with a few drops of purple gel food coloring, and dye the other half with double the amount of gel food coloring added to the first half.

Line a piping bag with a piping tip to pipe the Vanilla Buttercream onto the shells. Set aside. Next, make the Grape Jam. In a small saucepan, bring the grapes, sugar and lemon juice to a boil and let it simmer over medium heat for 15 to 20 minutes, until the grapes are falling apart. Use the back of a spoon to help mash the grapes. If the mixture starts to dry out or stick to the pan, lower the heat and add a tablespoon (15 ml) of water to the pan.

In a small bowl, combine the cornstarch and cold water. Once the grapes have fallen apart, add the cornstarch mixture to the pan and bring it to a simmer, stirring constantly for 1 or 2 minutes until the jam is very thick. Remove the pan from the heat and pour the jam into a bowl. Let it cool down, then cover it and place it in the fridge for about 2 hours until completely chilled.

To make the Vanilla Buttercream, beat the butter in a large bowl with a mixer on medium-high speed for 2 minutes until light and fluffy. With the mixer off, add the powdered sugar and cream to the bowl, and mix on low speed until the ingredients are incorporated. Once you no longer see dry streaks, beat the mixture on medium-high speed for 1 to 2 minutes, until fluffy and creamy. If the buttercream is too runny, add more powdered sugar, 1 tablespoon (8 g) at a time, and if the buttercream is too thick, add more cream, 1 teaspoon at a time, until the proper consistency is achieved. Add the vanilla and mix to combine. Transfer the buttercream to the prepared piping bag.

To assemble the macarons, pipe a ring of Vanilla Buttercream around the edges of each bottom shell. Spoon a bit of Grape Jam in the center of each macaron, and top with another shell. Let the macarons chill, covered, in the fridge overnight before serving, then let them sit at room temperature for 10 to 20 minutes before enjoying.

The Grape Macarons will store, covered, in the fridge for up to 5 days, or in the freezer, in an airtight container, for up to a month.

apricot macarons

You couldn't find a better complement to apricot preserves than the incredible French Vanilla Buttercream in these macarons. It's not overly sweet and gives the preserves a chance to shine their nectarous and rich flavor. The shells of the macarons are airbrushed lightly with orange food coloring, which makes me think of a sunset at the beach: the perfect setting for these dainty Apricot Macarons.

yield: 20 (1¹/₂" [4-cm]) macaron sandwiches

1 batch Plain Macaron Shells (page 24) dyed with a few drops of peach gel food coloring

french vanilla buttercream
6 tbsp (85 g) unsalted butter, softened
2 large egg yolks
3 tbsp (36 g) granulated sugar
1 tsp vanilla extract

for the filling
¹/₄ cup (80 g) apricot preserves

for decoration
Orange airbrush food coloring

tools
Piping bag
Round piping tip (¹/₄" [6 mm] in diameter) or piping tip of your choice
Candy thermometer
Airbrush machine (optional)

First, make the Plain Macaron Shells by following the directions on page 24 and adding a couple of drops of peach gel food coloring to the batter when instructed.

Line a piping bag with a piping tip to pipe the French Vanilla Buttercream on the shells. Set aside.

To make the French Vanilla Buttercream, remove the butter from the fridge 1 to 2 hours in advance. The butter needs to be softened, but not too soft, though it also shouldn't be cold. If the butter is too soft, the buttercream won't come together and will be too runny. If the butter is too cold, it will form lumps in the buttercream that won't incorporate with the frosting, and then you will be biting into chunks of butter when you eat it. The butter should be at around 68 to 72°F (20 to 22°C).

Place the egg yolks, sugar and vanilla in a heat-proof bowl. Set the bowl over a pot of barely simmering water to form a double boiler. Make sure the bottom of the bowl isn't touching the water, to prevent the yolks from cooking. Whisk the mixture for about 5 minutes, until it reaches 155°F (68°C) on a candy thermometer. Basically you are looking to melt the sugar granules, and also make the egg yolks safe for consumption.

Once the syrup is to temperature, remove the bowl from the double boiler, and begin to whip it with an electric mixer on medium speed until the yolk mixture has become fluffy with stiff peaks. This usually takes 7 to 8 minutes because the mixture has to cool down to start forming the peaks, but depending on your mixer, it can take even longer.

(continued)

Make sure the yolk mixture achieves stiff peaks. If the peaks are not stiff enough before you start to add the butter, the buttercream won't come together.

Cut the butter into 1-tablespoon (14-g) pats, and once the yolk mixture has reached stiff peaks, begin to add one pat of butter at a time, whisking it completely into the yolk mixture before adding the next slab of butter. This whole process could take up to 15 minutes.

Once you are done adding the butter, the buttercream should already be firming up and becoming thick and creamy. If at this point the buttercream isn't doing any of those things, it's either because the butter was too soft or the yolk mixture wasn't whipped enough. One way to troubleshoot it is to place the bowl in the fridge for 10 to 15 minutes, and then try to whip it again.

Once all of the butter has been incorporated, and the buttercream is creamy and smooth, transfer it to the prepared piping bag.

To decorate the macaron shells, place some orange food coloring in the airbrush machine and spray it lightly over the shells. Let the shells dry for 30 minutes or so.

To assemble the macarons, pipe a ring of French Vanilla Buttercream around the edges of each bottom shell. Spoon a bit of apricot preserves in the center of each macaron, and top with another shell.

Let the macarons chill, covered, in the fridge overnight before serving, then let them sit at room temperature for 10 to 20 minutes before enjoying.

The Apricot Macarons will store well, covered, in the fridge for up to 5 days, or in the freezer, in an airtight container, for up to a month.

white chocolate raspberry macarons

White chocolate and raspberry is a heavenly combination. The tartness of the raspberries is such a good complement to the sweetness of the white chocolate! And in this recipe, we are adding raspberries to the ganache itself, which will result in a creamy ganache with sharp fruity notes. To the center of the macarons, we have also added a bit of Raspberry Jam, for an extra memorable touch, adding to the sweet and sour harmony of this exceptional flavor combination.

yield: 20 (1½" [4-cm]) macaron sandwiches

1 batch Freeze-Dried Fruit Shells (page 36) using freeze-dried raspberry powder, dyed with a few drops of fuchsia gel food coloring

raspberry jam

1 cup (125 g) raspberries, fresh or frozen
3 tbsp (36 g) granulated sugar
1 tbsp (15 ml) lemon juice
2 tsp (5 g) cornstarch
1 tbsp (15 ml) cold water

raspberry white chocolate ganache

1 cup (170 g) chopped white chocolate (see Note)
⅔ cup (83 g) raspberries, fresh or frozen
¼ cup (60 ml) heavy cream

for decoration

⅓ cup (56 g) chopped white chocolate
¼ cup (24 g) freeze-dried raspberry powder

tools

Piping bag
Round piping tip (¼" [6 mm] in diameter) or piping tip of your choice

First, make the Freeze-Dried Fruit Shells by following the directions on page 36, adding freeze-dried raspberry powder to the dry ingredients and a few drops of fuchsia gel food coloring when instructed.

Line a piping bag with a piping tip to pipe the Raspberry White Chocolate Ganache onto the shells. Set aside.

Next, make the Raspberry Jam. In a small saucepan, bring the raspberries, sugar and lemon juice to a boil and let it simmer over medium heat for about 15 minutes, until the raspberries are falling apart. Use the back of a spoon to help mash the raspberries. If the mixture starts to dry out or stick to the pan, lower the heat and add a tablespoon (15 ml) of water to the pan.

In a small bowl, combine the cornstarch and cold water. Once the raspberries are soft and have fallen apart, add the cornstarch mixture to the pan and bring it to a simmer, stirring constantly for 1 or 2 minutes until the jam is very thick.

Remove the pan from the heat and pour the jam into a bowl. Let it cool down, then cover it and place it in the fridge for about 2 hours until completely chilled.

(continued)

white chocolate raspberry macarons
(continued)

To make the Raspberry White Chocolate Ganache, begin by placing the chocolate in a heat-proof bowl. Set it aside.

In a food processor or blender, puree the raspberries. Strain the puree through a fine-mesh sieve and discard the seeds. You should obtain a bit less than ¼ cup (60 ml).

In a small pan, bring the cream and the raspberry puree to a boil over medium heat, stirring occasionally to incorporate the ingredients. As soon as you see the first few bubbles, turn off the heat.

Pour the hot cream and raspberry mixture over the chocolate, then cover the bowl with a towel and let it sit for 1 minute. Use a whisk to gently incorporate the chocolate and cream mixture. Continue to whisk gently until the chocolate has completely melted. If you notice lumps of chocolate in the ganache, you can strain them out, or heat the bowl in the microwave for 5-second intervals, stirring in between to ensure all the bits of chocolate have melted. However, be careful to avoid overheating the chocolate so it doesn't become lumpy and thick.

Set the ganache aside to cool to room temperature. It will thicken as it cools down. After about 2 hours, the ganache should have a good piping consistency. If it is still too soft, place it in the fridge for 10 to 20 minutes, and give it a good stir before transferring it to the prepared piping bag.

To decorate the top shells, place the chocolate in a small heat-proof bowl and microwave it for 15-second intervals, stirring in between, until completely melted. Dip the top of 20 shells in the melted chocolate, and place them on a baking sheet. While the chocolate is still wet, top the shells with freeze-dried raspberry powder.

To assemble the macarons, pipe a ring of Raspberry White Chocolate Ganache around the edges of each bottom shell, then spoon some Raspberry Jam in the center. Top with a decorated shell.

Let the macarons chill, covered, in the fridge overnight before serving, then let them sit at room temperature for 10 to 20 minutes before enjoying.

The White Chocolate Raspberry Macarons will store well, covered, in the fridge for up to 5 days, or in the freezer, in an airtight container, for up to a month.

note: Be sure to use real white chocolate made with at least 20 percent cocoa butter. If the ganache separates or curdles, add a tablespoon (15 ml) of cream to it, place it over a double boiler and gently stir until it comes back together. It might need another tablespoon (15 ml) of cream to do so. Continue to gently stir the ganache until it becomes slightly warm, then let it cool down again before using.

strawberry kiwi macarons

These Strawberry Kiwi Macarons are cheery, colorful and will brighten your day! The shells are strawberry flavored and filled with a delicious, slightly tart Kiwi Jam, and a fluffy Strawberry Buttercream. The kiwi and strawberry combination is a match made in heaven that's bursting with sweetness and subtle tartness. These macarons offer a tropical explosion in every bite.

yield: 20 (1½" [4-cm]) macaron sandwiches

1 batch Freeze-Dried Fruit Macaron Shells (page 36) using freeze-dried strawberry powder and dyed with pink gel food coloring

kiwi jam
¾ cup (112 g) chopped kiwi
2 tbsp (25 g) granulated sugar
2 tbsp (30 ml) lemon juice
2 tsp (5 g) cornstarch
1 tbsp (15 ml) cold water

strawberry buttercream
4 tbsp (56 g) unsalted butter, at room temperature
1½ cups (188 g) powdered sugar, sifted, plus more as needed
⅓ cup (30 g) freeze-dried strawberry powder
2 tbsp (30 ml) milk, as needed

for decoration
2½ tbsp (28 g) white chocolate, chopped
¼ cup (38 g) sprinkles (optional)

tools
2 piping bags
Round piping tip (¼" [6 mm] in diameter) or piping tip of your choice

First, make the Freeze-Dried Fruit Macaron Shells, following the directions on page 36, adding freeze-dried strawberry powder to the dry ingredients and a few drops of pink gel food coloring when instructed. Line a piping bag with a piping tip for the Strawberry Buttercream. Set aside.

Next, make the Kiwi Jam. In a small saucepan, bring the kiwi, sugar and lemon juice to a boil and let it simmer over medium heat for about 15 minutes, until the kiwi is falling apart. Use a spoon to help mash the kiwi. If the mixture starts to dry out, lower the heat and add a tablespoon (15 ml) of water to the pan.

In a small bowl, combine the cornstarch and cold water. Once the kiwi has fallen apart, add the cornstarch mixture to the pan and bring it to a simmer, stirring constantly for 1 or 2 minutes until the jam is very thick. Remove the pan from the heat and pour the jam into a bowl. Let it cool down, then cover it and place it in the fridge for about 2 hours until completely chilled.

To make the Strawberry Buttercream, beat the butter in a large bowl with a mixer on medium-high speed for 2 minutes until light and fluffy. With the mixer off, add the powdered sugar and freeze-dried strawberry powder to the bowl, and mix on low speed until the ingredients are incorporated. Once you no longer see dry streaks, beat the mixture on medium-high speed for 1 to 2 minutes, until creamy and smooth. If the buttercream is too runny, add more powdered sugar, 1 tablespoon (8 g) at a time, and if the buttercream is too thick, add milk to thin it out, 1 teaspoon at a time. Transfer the buttercream to the prepared piping bag.

To assemble the macarons, pipe a ring of the Strawberry Buttercream around the edges of each bottom shell. Then, spoon some of the Kiwi Jam in the center of each macaron, and top with another shell. To decorate, place the white chocolate in a small heat-proof bowl and microwave for 15-second intervals, stirring in between, until melted. Transfer the chocolate to a piping bag, snip the end and drizzle over the macarons. Top with sprinkles if you'd like.

Let the macarons chill, covered, in the fridge overnight before serving, then let them sit at room temperature for 10 to 20 minutes before enjoying. The Strawberry Kiwi Macarons will store well, covered, in the fridge for up to 5 days, or in the freezer, in an airtight container, for up to a month.

starburst macarons

These vibrant Starburst® Macarons will bring you to a state of sheer bliss. They are filled with an easy to make Starburst Buttercream that is literally bursting with sweet candy flavor! You can use pretty much any soft chewy fruity candy to make the filling for the macarons, though I especially love using Starbursts because they are so sweet and pleasantly fruity. These Starburst Macarons are nostalgic for many, and the fun colors and bright flavors will remind you of simpler times!

yield: 20 (1½" [4-cm]) macaron sandwiches

1 batch Plain Macaron Shells (page 24) made using the Multicolored Shells technique demonstrated on page 148. Divide the batter into four portions and dye each portion a different color: orange, red, pink and yellow.

starburst buttercream

10 Starburst candies (45 g)

2 tbsp (30 ml) heavy cream, plus more as needed

4 tbsp (56 g) unsalted butter, at room temperature

1½ cups (187 g) powdered sugar, sifted, plus more as needed

tools

Piping bag

Large open star piping tip (⅓" [1 cm] in diameter) or piping tip of your choice

First, make the Plain Macaron Shells according to the directions on page 24. Follow the instructions on page 148 of the Decorating Techniques chapter to make the multicolor shells. For this recipe, the batter is divided into four portions and each portion is dyed a different color: orange, red, pink and yellow.

Line a piping bag with a piping tip to pipe the Starburst Buttercream onto the shells. Set aside.

To make the Starburst Buttercream, heat the Starbursts in a small bowl in the microwave for about 5 seconds, then add the cream and return the bowl to the microwave. Microwave for 5-second intervals, stirring in between, until the Starbursts have melted with the cream to form a smooth mixture. Keep in mind that if you microwave the Starbursts for too long, they will burn and stick, so it's important to be patient and go slowly when doing this.

Once the Starbursts and cream are combined, set the mixture aside to cool for about 20 minutes.

Meanwhile, beat the butter in a large bowl with a mixer on medium-high speed for 2 minutes until light and fluffy. With the mixer off, add the powdered sugar and cooled Starburst mixture to the bowl, and mix on low speed until the ingredients are incorporated. Once you no longer see streaks of dry powdered sugar, beat the mixture on medium-high speed for 1 to 2 minutes, until creamy and fluffy. If the buttercream is too runny, add more powdered sugar as needed, 1 tablespoon (8 g) at a time, and if the buttercream is too thick, add more cream to thin it out, 1 teaspoon at a time, until the proper consistency is achieved. Transfer the buttercream to the prepared piping bag.

To assemble the macarons, pipe the Starburst Buttercream on each bottom shell, then top with another shell.

Let the macarons chill, covered, in the fridge overnight before serving, then let them sit at room temperature for 10 to 20 minutes before enjoying.

The Starburst Macarons will store well, covered, in the fridge for up to 5 days, or in the freezer, in an airtight container, for up to a month.

tart and citrusy

The sunny macarons in this chapter will absolutely lift you up and cure your blues. They feature vibrant and lovely fillings that are a mix of sweet, sour and tangy. Fruits such as lemon, pomegranate, orange, seasonal cranberry and exotic varieties such as passionfruit and cassis are the stars of the show in the following recipes. Some are soothing and floral like the Lemon Lavender Macarons (page 125) or the Orange Rose Macarons (page 120), and others are electrifying, such as the Pomegranate Dark Chocolate Macarons (page 108) and the Ruby Passionfruit Macarons (page 111).

mojito macarons

Here we have zesty lime shells filled with a delicious Mojito Buttercream that is flavored with refreshing chopped mint, rum, lime juice and lime zest. The rum taste is very subtle and adds a bit of spice and richness to the buttercream. The chopped mint can be substituted for mint extract, but I prefer the fresh mint, as it's less overpowering and gives a natural herbal taste to the macarons. The lime adds a much-needed tartness that cuts through the sweet buttercream, making it lively and enjoyable.

yield: 20 (1½" [4-cm]) macaron sandwiches

1 batch Citrus Zest Macaron Shells (page 37) made with lime zest and a few drops of green gel food coloring

mojito buttercream

6 tbsp (85 g) unsalted butter, at room temperature

2 cups (250 g) powdered sugar, sifted, plus more as needed

1 tbsp (15 ml) white rum or 1 tsp vanilla extract

1 tbsp (15 ml) lime juice

1 tbsp (5 g) lime zest

¼ tsp finely chopped fresh mint (1–2 leaves) or ¼ tsp mint extract

½ tbsp (7 ml) milk or water, as needed

for decoration

1 drop green gel food coloring

Few drops water or clear liquor

tools

Piping bag

Large star piping tip (⅓" [1 cm] in diameter) or piping tip of your choice

Small food-safe brush

First, make the Citrus Zest Macaron Shells by following the directions on page 37 and adding lime zest and a few drops of green gel food coloring when instructed.

Line a piping bag with a piping tip to pipe the Mojito Buttercream onto the shells. Set aside.

To make the Mojito Buttercream, beat the butter in a large bowl with a mixer on medium-high speed for 2 minutes until fluffy. Add the powdered sugar, rum, lime juice, lime zest and mint to the bowl, and mix on low speed until the ingredients are incorporated. Once you no longer see streaks of dry powdered sugar, beat the mixture on medium-high speed for 1 to 2 minutes, until creamy and fluffy. If the buttercream is too runny, add more powdered sugar as needed, 1 tablespoon (8 g) at a time, and if the buttercream is too thick, add milk, water or more rum to thin it out, 1 teaspoon at a time, until the proper consistency is achieved. Transfer the buttercream to the prepared piping bag.

To decorate the shells, mix the food coloring with the water until the food coloring is dissolved. Dip a brush in the mixture and brush it on top of the shells.

To assemble the macarons, pipe the Mojito Buttercream on each bottom shell, and then top with another shell.

Let the macarons chill, covered, in the fridge overnight before serving, then let them sit at room temperature for 10 to 20 minutes before enjoying.

The Mojito Macarons will store well, covered, in the fridge for up to 5 days, or in the freezer, in an airtight container, for up to a month.

pomegranate dark chocolate macarons

There is something so romantic about the combination of pomegranate and dark chocolate. A taste of these macarons might just give you butterflies! The sweet and slightly tart Pomegranate Curd enveloped by a rich Dark Chocolate Ganache makes for a luscious filling that will delight your senses.

yield: 20 (1½" [4-cm]) macaron sandwiches

1 batch Plain Macaron Shells (page 24) dyed with a few drops of mauve gel food coloring

pomegranate curd
1 tbsp (5 g) dried hibiscus (optional, see Note)
¼ cup (50 g) granulated sugar
2 tbsp (28 g) unsalted butter, at room temperature
3 large egg yolks
⅓ cup (78 ml) pomegranate juice
1 tbsp (15 ml) lemon juice

dark chocolate ganache
1 cup (170 g) finely chopped dark chocolate
½ cup (120 ml) heavy cream

for decoration
3 tbsp (30 g) dark chocolate
¼ cup (38 g) pomegranate seeds

tools
2 piping bags
Round piping tip (¼" [6 mm] in diameter) or piping tip of your choice
Candy thermometer

First, make the Plain Macaron Shells, following the directions on page 24 and adding a few drops of mauve gel food coloring when instructed.

Line a piping bag with a piping tip to pipe the Dark Chocolate Ganache onto the shells. Set aside.

To make the Pomegranate Curd, pulse the dried hibiscus (if using) and sugar in a small blender or food processor until the hibiscus is finely ground.

To the bowl of a mixer, add the butter, egg yolks and hibiscus sugar. Beat the ingredients for just 1 minute. Slowly add the pomegranate juice and the lemon juice to the bowl, mixing to combine. The mixture won't be nicely incorporated or smooth yet, and that's okay.

Transfer the mixture to a small saucepan with a heavy bottom and heat it over medium-low heat, stirring constantly. Don't let the mixture come to a boil. It will quickly become very liquid, and then it will start to heat up and thicken. Use a candy thermometer to continually take the temperature of the curd. Remove the pan from the heat once it reaches 170°F (76°C). Transfer the curd to a bowl, straining it to remove any bits of cooked egg and larger pieces of hibiscus flower. Place the curd in the fridge to chill for 1 hour before using.

While the curd chills, make the Dark Chocolate Ganache. Begin by placing the chocolate in a heat-proof bowl. Set it aside.

Heat the cream in a small pan over medium heat, or in a small bowl in the microwave, until it almost comes to a boil. This should take a couple of minutes in the saucepan and about 30 seconds in the microwave.

(continued)

pomegranate dark chocolate macarons (continued)

Pour the hot cream over the chocolate and let the mixture stand for 1 minute. Then, use a whisk to gently incorporate the chocolate and the cream. Continue to whisk gently until the chocolate has completely melted. If you notice lumps of chocolate in the ganache, you can strain them out, or heat the bowl in the microwave for 5-second intervals, stirring in between to ensure all the bits of chocolate have melted. However, be careful to avoid overheating the chocolate so it doesn't become lumpy and thick.

Set the ganache aside to cool to room temperature or until it has a good piping consistency. You can place the ganache in the fridge for about 10 minutes, stirring every so often, if you'd prefer to speed things up. If the ganache gets too hard, microwave it for 3- to 5-second intervals, stirring in between to obtain a smooth, spreadable consistency. Keep in mind that if you heat it up too much, the ganache can become too liquid or even separate. When you have reached the desired consistency, transfer the ganache to the prepared piping bag.

To decorate the top shells, place the chocolate in a small heat-proof bowl and microwave it for 15-second intervals, stirring in between, until completely melted.

Transfer it to a piping bag, snip the end with scissors and drizzle melted chocolate over 20 of the shells. While the chocolate is still wet, place some pomegranate seeds on top so that they will stick to the shells.

To assemble the macarons, pipe a ring of Dark Chocolate Ganache around the edges of each bottom shell. Spoon some of the Pomegranate Curd in the middle, and top with a decorated shell.

Let the macarons chill, covered, in the fridge overnight before serving, then let them sit at room temperature for 10 to 20 minutes before enjoying.

These Pomegranate Dark Chocolate Macarons will store well, covered, in the fridge for up to 5 days, or in the freezer, in an airtight container, for up to a month.

note: The dried hibiscus is optional, but it will preserve the Pomegranate Curd's vibrant red color and prevent it from turning brown as it cooks. You can easily find dried hibiscus on Amazon, and any online or in-person tea stores.

ruby passionfruit macarons

Ruby chocolate is a naturally pink chocolate, made from ruby cocoa beans, that tastes fruity and lusciously tangy. The perfect pairing for ruby chocolate is passionfruit, because of their similar notes, which become enhanced when they are combined. These Ruby Passionfruit Macarons are filled with a sweet and pleasantly tart Ruby Ganache, as well as a very aromatic and refreshing Passionfruit Curd.

yield: 20 (1¹/₂" [4-cm]) macaron sandwiches

1 batch Plain Macaron Shells (page 24) made using the Multicolored Shells technique for two-tone shells demonstrated on page 148. Dye half the batter with a few drops of yellow gel food coloring, and dye the other half with a mix of pink and mauve gel food coloring.

passionfruit curd

3 tbsp (42 g) unsalted butter, at room temperature

3 tbsp (36 g) granulated sugar

2 large egg yolks

¹/₄ cup (60 ml) passionfruit pulp (see Note)

1 tbsp (15 ml) lemon juice

ruby ganache

1 cup plus 3 tbsp (200 g) chopped ruby chocolate

¹/₃ cup (78 ml) heavy cream

tools

Piping bag

Round piping tip (¹/₄" [6 mm] in diameter) or piping tip of your choice

Candy thermometer

First, make the Plain Macaron Shells by following the directions on page 24. Follow the instructions on page 148 of the Decorating Techniques chapter to make the two-toned shells. For this recipe, half the batter was dyed with a few drops of yellow gel food coloring, and the other half was dyed with a mix of pink and mauve gel food coloring.

Line a piping bag with a piping tip to pipe the Ruby Ganache onto the shells. Set aside.

To make the Passionfruit Curd, beat the butter and the sugar with an electric mixer for 30 seconds until incorporated. Add the yolks and mix until combined. Next, add the passionfruit pulp and lemon juice and mix briefly.

After adding the passionfruit and lemon juice to the bowl, the mixture may seem separated and chunky, and that's okay. Transfer the mixture to a small saucepan with a heavy bottom, and heat it over low heat, stirring constantly. Don't let the mixture come to a boil. Keep the heat very low, and don't stop stirring.

Continue cooking for 5 to 10 minutes, until the curd is thick enough to coat the back of a spoon. Use a candy thermometer to continually take the temperature of the curd. Remove the pan from the heat once it reaches 170°F (76°C). Transfer the curd to a bowl, straining it to remove any bits of cooked egg. Place the curd in the fridge to chill for a few hours before using.

To make the Ruby Ganache, begin by placing the chocolate in a heat-proof bowl. Set it aside.

(continued)

ruby passionfruit macarons (continued)

Heat the cream in a small saucepan over medium heat, or in a small bowl in the microwave, until it almost comes to a boil. This should take a couple of minutes in the saucepan and about 30 seconds in the microwave Then, pour the hot cream over the chocolate. Cover the bowl with a plate or towel and let it sit for 1 minute, then stir with a spatula until the chocolate has melted entirely. Set the ganache aside until it cools to room temperature. It will thicken as it cools down. Once the Ruby Ganache is at room temperature, it should be thick, creamy and spreadable. Transfer it to the prepared piping bag.

To assemble the macarons, pipe a ring of ganache around the edges of the bottom shells. Spoon some of the Passionfruit Curd in the middle of each macaron, and top with another shell.

Let the macarons chill, covered, in the fridge overnight before serving, and let them sit at room temperature for 10 to 20 minutes before enjoying.

The Ruby Passionfruit Macarons will store well, covered, in the fridge for up to 5 days, or in the freezer, in an airtight container, for up to a month.

note: Look for passionfruit pulp that doesn't have any sugar added, or else the curd will be too sweet. If you can't find fresh passionfruit at your local grocery store, you can easily find the pulp in the frozen aisle of most grocery stores, or online.

cranberry white chocolate macarons

These pretty-in-pink macarons are filled with a tart and tangy Cranberry Curd surrounded by a rich and luscious White Chocolate Ganache. They are perfect for end-of-the-year celebrations, when cranberries are in season, but can be made all year round if you can find frozen cranberries. White chocolate and cranberry is such a classic and festive combination, and the addition of these macarons will elevate your cookie boxes and holiday spreads.

yield: 20 (1¹/₂" [4-cm]) macaron sandwiches

1 batch Plain Macaron Shells (page 24) dyed with a few drops of mauve gel food coloring

cranberry curd
¹/₂ cup (75 g) cranberries, fresh or frozen
3 tbsp (45 ml) water
1 large egg yolk
2 tbsp (25 g) granulated sugar
1 tbsp (14 g) unsalted butter, at room temperature

white chocolate ganache
1 cup (170 g) chopped white chocolate (see Note)
¹/₃ cup (78 ml) heavy cream

for decoration
2¹/₂ tbsp (28 g) chopped white chocolate

tools
2 piping bags
Round piping tip (¹/₄" [6 mm] in diameter) or piping tip of your choice
Candy thermometer

First, make the Plain Macaron Shells, following the directions on page 24 and adding a few drops of mauve gel food coloring to the batter when instructed.

Line a piping bag with a piping tip to pipe the White Chocolate Ganache onto the shells. Set aside.

To make the Cranberry Curd, bring the cranberries and water to a boil in a small saucepan over medium heat. Let the cranberries simmer for 5 minutes, stirring constantly and using the back of a spatula to pop the cranberries as they soften. If the mixture gets too dry, add another tablespoon (15 ml) of water. Remove the pan from the heat, and transfer the mixture to a bowl, straining it through a sieve. Press down to extract as much liquid as possible. Discard the cranberry skins.

Meanwhile, whisk the yolk and sugar together in a bowl. Add the butter and continue to whisk until smooth. Slowly pour the cranberry juice into the bowl, whisking constantly. Once everything is incorporated, pour the mixture into a small saucepan. Slowly heat the mixture over medium-low heat, stirring constantly. Don't turn up the heat too high, or the egg will scramble.

(continued)

cranberry white chocolate macarons
(continued)

Continue to cook over medium-low heat for 5 to 10 minutes until the curd thickens. Use a candy thermometer to continually take the temperature of the curd. Remove the pan from the heat once it reaches 170°F (76°C). Transfer the curd to a bowl, and place it in the fridge to chill completely before using.

While the curd chills, make the White Chocolate Ganache. Begin by placing the chocolate in a glass or stainless steel bowl. Set it aside.

Heat the cream in a small pan over medium heat, or in a small bowl in the microwave, until it almost comes to a boil. This should take a couple of minutes in the saucepan and about 30 seconds in the microwave.

Pour the hot cream over the chocolate and cover the bowl with a plate or towel, then let the mixture stand for 1 minute. Use a whisk to gently incorporate the chocolate and the cream. Continue to whisk gently until the chocolate has completely melted.

Set the ganache aside to cool to room temperature or until it has a good piping consistency.

Once the White Chocolate Ganache is at room temperature, it should be thick, creamy and spreadable. Transfer it to the prepared piping bag.

To decorate the top shells, place the chocolate in a small heat-proof bowl and microwave it for 15-second intervals, stirring in between, until completely melted. Transfer the melted chocolate to a piping bag, use scissors to snip the end and drizzle chocolate over 20 of the shells.

To assemble the macarons, pipe a ring of ganache around the edges of the bottom shells. Spoon some of the Cranberry Curd in the middle of each macaron, and top with a decorated shell.

Let the macarons chill, covered, in the fridge overnight before serving, then let them sit at room temperature for 10 to 20 minutes before enjoying.

The Cranberry White Chocolate Macarons will store well, covered, in the fridge for up to 5 days, or in the freezer, in an airtight container, for up to a month.

note: Be sure to use real white chocolate made with at least 20 percent cocoa butter. If the ganache separates or curdles, add a tablespoon (15 ml) of cream to it, place it over a double boiler and gently stir until it comes back together. It might need another tablespoon (15 ml) of cream to do so. Continue to gently stir the ganache until it becomes slightly warm, then let it cool down again before using.

cassis macarons

These Cassis Macarons are filled with a Cassis Italian Buttercream and black currant jam. Black currant jam is slightly tart, with a tannic finish and a bit of sweetness, while the Cassis Italian Buttercream is super fluffy, light and also not overly sweet. These are perfect for people who prefer macarons on the less sweet side.

yield: 20 (1½" [4-cm]) macaron sandwiches

1 batch Plain Macaron Shells (page 24) dyed with a few drops of mauve and purple gel food coloring

cassis italian buttercream

½ cup (113 g) unsalted butter, softened
1/3 cup (80 g) black currant jam
1½ tbsp (22 ml) plus 1 tsp water, divided
1 large egg white (40 g)
Pinch of cream of tartar
⅓ cup (66 g) granulated sugar, divided
½ tsp vanilla extract

for the filling

¼ cup (60 g) black currant jam

for decoration

½ cup (85 g) chopped white chocolate

tools

2 piping bags
Open star piping tip (¼" [6 mm] in diameter) or piping tip of your choice
Candy thermometer

First, make the Plain Macaron Shells, following the directions on page 24 and adding a few drops of mauve and purple gel food coloring to the batter when instructed.

Line a piping bag with a piping tip to pipe the Cassis Italian Buttercream onto the shells. Set aside.

To make the Cassis Italian Buttercream, remove the butter from the fridge 1 to 2 hours in advance. The butter needs to be softened, but not too soft, though it also shouldn't be cold. If the butter is too soft, the buttercream won't come together and will be too runny. If the butter is too cold, it will form lumps in the buttercream that won't incorporate with the frosting, and then you will be biting into chunks of butter when you eat it. The butter should be at around 68 to 72°F (20 to 22°C).

Combine the black currant jam with 1 teaspoon of water in a small bowl. Microwave the mixture for 10 seconds, give it a good stir and then pour it through a strainer, using a spatula to squeeze the jam and remove as much liquid as possible. You should end up with about 3 tablespoons (45 ml) of liquid. This will be used later in the buttercream. Set the liquid aside and discard the solids.

In the bowl of a small mixer or with a hand mixer, whip the egg white and cream of tartar on medium-low speed. Once you see the mixture foam up, add 1 tablespoon (15 g) of sugar to the bowl. You are looking to whip the white just until soft peaks form. It's best not to use a stand mixer when whipping a single egg white, because the whisk won't reach the bottom of the bowl. If you prefer using a stand mixer, you can double the recipe (and end up with leftovers that can be frozen for up to 2 months).

(continued)

At the same time that the egg white is whipping, mix the remaining sugar (⅓ cup minus 1 tablespoon [51 g]) along with 1½ tablespoons (22 ml) of water in a small saucepan over medium heat, just until combined. Clip a candy thermometer to the side of the pan, making sure the tip of the thermometer is submerged in the syrup but not touching the bottom of the pan. This is a very small amount of sugar and water, so if the saucepan is too big, the height of the syrup won't be enough to accurately tell the temperature with a candy thermometer, and it's very important to get an accurate temperature reading.

Without stirring the syrup, let it come to a boil. Cook for a few minutes until it reaches 235°F (113°C).

The syrup should reach 235°F (113°C) at the same time that the meringue achieves soft peaks. Immediately as this happens, reduce the mixer speed to low, remove the syrup from the heat and pour it in a steady stream over the whipped egg white.

Increase the mixer speed to medium-high, and continue to whip the meringue until stiff peaks form. It may take anywhere from 10 to 15 minutes, or even longer depending on your mixer, since the syrup will be pretty hot. It's very important to continue whipping until the meringue is no longer warm and the peaks are firm.

Once the meringue has achieved stiff peaks and cooled down, start adding the butter, one tablespoon (14 g) at a time, whisking each piece completely into the meringue before adding the next. After all the butter has been added, continue to whip on medium-high speed until the meringue becomes creamy and fluffy. If it looks watered down and separated, just continue to whip and be patient.

This can take anywhere from 5 to 10 minutes. If the buttercream looks too soupy and runny, it's probably either because the butter was too soft or the meringue wasn't whipped enough. One way to troubleshoot it is to place the bowl in the fridge for about 10 minutes, and then try to whip it again. If it's still not working, repeat this, and leave it in the fridge for longer, then resume whipping.

Once the buttercream is fluffy, creamy, and stiff, add the vanilla and strained jam. Mix on medium speed to incorporate. Transfer the Cassis Italian Buttercream to the prepared piping bag.

To decorate the top shells, place the chocolate in a small heat-proof bowl and microwave it for 15-second intervals, stirring in between, until completely melted. Transfer the melted chocolate to a piping bag, use scissors to snip the end and drizzle chocolate over 20 of the shells. I did a swirl pattern on top of the shells.

To assemble the macarons, pipe a ring of Cassis Italian Buttercream around the edges of each bottom shell. Spoon some black currant jam in the center of each macaron, and then top with a decorated shell.

Let the macarons chill, covered, in the fridge overnight before serving, then let them sit at room temperature for 10 to 20 minutes before enjoying.

The Cassis Macarons will store well, covered, in the fridge for up to 5 days, or in the freezer, in an airtight container, for up to a month.

orange rose macarons

Rose is a very polarizing flavor—people either love it or can't go near it. And that's because it has to be done right. When it comes to using rose as a flavor, a little goes a very, very long way. Orange pairs extraordinarily well with rose; its fruity flavor offsets the strong rose fragrance, leaving a subtle floral aroma that adds a rich sensory experience to these macarons.

yield: 20 (1½" [4-cm]) macaron sandwiches

1 batch Plain Macaron Shells (page 24) dyed with a few drops of pink gel food coloring

orange marmalade

1 cup (180 g) oranges, peeled and diced small
¼ cup (50 g) granulated sugar
3–6 tbsp (45–90 ml) water
1 tbsp (5 g) orange zest

rose buttercream

6 tbsp (85 g) unsalted butter, at room temperature
1–1½ cups (125–187 g) powdered sugar, sifted
1 tbsp (15 ml) heavy cream, as needed
1 tbsp (5 g) orange zest
⅛ tsp rose water

for decoration

½ cup (85 g) chopped white chocolate
3 tbsp (30 g) edible rose petals

tools
Piping bag
Open star piping tip (¼" [6 mm] in diameter) or piping tip of your choice

First, make the Plain Macaron Shells, following the directions on page 24 and adding a few drops of pink gel food coloring to the batter when instructed.

Line a piping bag with a piping tip to pipe the Rose Buttercream onto the shells. Set aside. Next, make the Orange Marmalade. In a small saucepan, bring the oranges, sugar, 3 tablespoons (45 ml) of water and the orange zest to a boil. Once it starts boiling, reduce the heat to low and let it simmer for about 40 minutes. If the mixture starts to dry out or stick to the pan, lower the heat and add the remaining water to the pan.

When it's ready, the marmalade will be very fragrant, sticky, syrupy and thick. Remove the pan from the heat, and transfer the marmalade to a bowl. Let it cool down, then cover it and place it in the fridge for about 2 hours until completely chilled.

To make the Rose Buttercream beat the butter in a large bowl with a mixer on medium-high speed for 2 minutes until fluffy. Add 1 cup (125 g) of powdered sugar, and mix on low speed until the ingredients are incorporated. Once you no longer see streaks of dry powdered sugar, beat the mixture on medium-high speed for 1 to 2 minutes, until creamy and fluffy. If the buttercream is too runny, add more powdered sugar, 1 tablespoon (8 g) at a time, and if the buttercream is too thick, add cream, 1 teaspoon at a time, until the proper consistency is achieved. Add the orange zest and rose water and mix to combine. Transfer the buttercream to the prepared piping bag.

To decorate the top shells, place the chocolate in a small heat-proof bowl and microwave it for 15-second intervals, stirring in between, until completely melted. I dipped the tops of some of the shells in the melted chocolate, then I drizzled melted chocolate over other macaron shells. Place mini food-grade dried rose buds or dried rose petals over the melted chocolate.

To assemble the macarons, pipe the Rose Buttercream onto each bottom shell, and then top with a decorated shell. Let the macarons chill, covered, in the fridge overnight before serving, then let them sit at room temperature for 10 to 20 minutes before enjoying.

The Orange Rose Macarons will store well, covered, in the fridge for up to 5 days, or in the freezer, in an airtight container, for up to a month.

lemon meringue macarons

Bright lemon shells, filled with a sweet and tangy Lemon Curd and gooey Marshmallow Frosting—these are like sunshine in macaron form! The Lemon Curd certainly packs a punch of flavor. It's sweet and has a sharp finish that will leave you wanting even more! The fluffy Marshmallow Frosting complements the bold lemon flavor so well.

yield: 20 (1¹⁄₂" [4-cm]) macaron sandwiches

1 batch Citrus Zest Macaron Shells (page 37) made with lemon zest and a few drops of yellow gel food coloring

lemon curd
3 tbsp (42 g) unsalted butter, at room temperature
3 tbsp (36 g) granulated sugar
2 large egg yolks
¹⁄₄ cup (60 ml) lemon juice
3 tbsp (15 g) lemon zest

marshmallow frosting
2 egg whites (60 g total)
¹⁄₂ cup (100 g) granulated sugar
¹⁄₄ tsp cream of tartar
¹⁄₈ tsp fine sea salt
1 tsp vanilla extract

tools
Piping bag
Round piping tip (¹⁄₄" [6 mm] in diameter) or piping tip of your choice
Candy thermometer
Kitchen torch (optional)

First, make the Citrus Zest Macaron Shells, following the directions on page 37. Add lemon zest to the dry ingredients, and add a few drops of yellow gel food coloring to the batter when instructed.

Line a piping bag with a piping tip to pipe the Marshmallow Frosting onto the shells. Set aside.

To make the Lemon Curd, beat the butter and sugar with an electric mixer for 30 seconds until incorporated. Add the yolks and mix until combined. Then, add the lemon juice and lemon zest to the bowl and mix briefly.

After adding the lemon juice to the bowl, the mixture may seem separated and chunky, and that's okay. Transfer the mixture to a small saucepan with a heavy bottom, and heat it over low heat, stirring constantly. Don't let the mixture come to a boil. Keep the heat very low, and don't stop stirring.

Continue cooking for 5 to 10 minutes, until the curd is thick enough to coat the back of a spoon. Use a candy thermometer to continually take the temperature of the curd. Remove the pan from the heat once it reaches 170°F (76°C). Transfer the curd to a bowl, straining it to remove any bits of cooked egg. Place the curd in the fridge to chill for a few hours before using.

To make the Marshmallow Frosting, combine the egg whites, sugar, cream of tartar and salt in a heat-proof bowl. Set the bowl over a pot of barely simmering water to form a double boiler. Make sure the bottom of the bowl isn't touching the water, to prevent the whites from cooking.

(continued)

lemon meringue macarons (continued)

Whisk the mixture for a few minutes until it reaches 140°F (60°C) on a candy thermometer. Once the syrup is to temperature, remove the bowl from the double boiler. Whip the syrup with an electric mixer fitted with a whisk attachment for about 5 minutes on high speed. Add the vanilla and mix to combine. By this point, the meringue should have firm peaks and be fluffy and glossy. If not, continue to whip, as some mixers might take longer to get there. Transfer the frosting to the prepared piping bag. The Marshmallow Frosting has to be piped immediately after being made. It will hold up nicely after it is piped, but if you don't pipe it right away, it will begin to deflate and become runny.

To assemble the macarons, pipe a ring of Marshmallow Frosting around the edges of each bottom shell. You can use a kitchen torch to toast the Marshmallow Frosting, to give it a nutty, caramelized flavor. Then, spoon some Lemon Curd in the center of each macaron, and top with another shell.

Let the macarons chill, covered, in the fridge overnight before serving, then let them sit at room temperature for 10 to 20 minutes before enjoying.

The Lemon Meringue Macarons will store well, covered, in the fridge for up to 5 days, or in the freezer, in an airtight container, for up to a month.

lemon lavender macarons

These exquisite lavender infused shells are filled with a Honey Lavender Buttercream, that is rich and aromatic, and a Lemon Lavender Curd. Infusing the curd with lavender gives it gorgeous floral notes. The lavender is not overpowering, and lends a delicate touch to the macarons. It brings out the floral taste in the honey from the buttercream, and contrasts nicely with the pungent lemon sourness, forming an elegant combo that will exceed all your expectations.

yield: 20 (1½" [4-cm]) macaron sandwiches

1 batch Lavender Macaron Shells (page 32). Refer to the Painting the Bag Technique instructions on page 150 to color the batter with a few drops of purple gel food coloring.

lemon lavender curd

3 tbsp (42 g) unsalted butter, at room temperature

3 tbsp (36 g) granulated sugar

2 large egg yolks

¼ cup (60 ml) lemon juice

3 tbsp (15 g) lemon zest

1 tsp food-grade dried lavender buds

honey lavender buttercream

3 tbsp (45 ml) milk, plus more as needed

1 tbsp (2 g) food-grade dried lavender buds

4 tbsp (56 g) unsalted butter, at room temperature

2 tbsp (30 ml) honey

2 cups (250 g) powdered sugar, sifted, plus more as needed

½ tsp vanilla extract

tools

Piping bag

Round piping tip (¼" [6 mm] in diameter) or piping tip of your choice

Candy thermometer

First, make the Lavender Macaron Shells, following the directions on page 32. Follow the instructions on page 150 of the Decorating Techniques chapter to dye the batter by painting the piping bag with a few drops of purple gel food coloring. This will create the slightly darker swirl on the shells that you see in the photo on page 127.

Line a piping bag with a piping tip to pipe the Honey Lavender Buttercream onto the shells. Set aside.

To make the Lemon Lavender Curd, beat the butter and sugar in a large bowl with an electric mixer for 30 seconds until incorporated. Add the yolks and mix until combined. Then, add the lemon juice and lemon zest to the bowl and mix briefly.

After adding the lemon juice to the bowl, the mixture may seem separated and chunky, and that's okay. Transfer the mixture to a small saucepan with a heavy bottom, add the lavender buds and heat it over low heat, stirring constantly. Don't let the mixture come to a boil. Keep the heat very low, and don't stop stirring.

Continue cooking for 5 to 10 minutes, until the curd is thick enough to coat the back of a spoon. Use a candy thermometer to continually take the temperature of the curd. Remove the pan from the heat once it reaches 170°F (76°C). Transfer the curd to a bowl, straining it to remove any bits of cooked egg and dried lavender. Place the curd in the fridge to chill for a few hours before using.

(continued)

lemon lavender macarons (continued)

To make the Honey Lavender Buttercream, begin by infusing the milk with lavender. Combine the milk and lavender buds in a small bowl and microwave it for 10-second intervals until very hot, but don't let the milk boil over. Set it aside to cool down completely.

Once the milk has cooled down, strain it and discard the lavender buds. Then, in a large bowl, beat the butter at medium speed for 1 minute. Add the honey, powdered sugar, infused milk and vanilla to the bowl. Mix on low speed until combined, then increase the speed to medium and continue to beat for 1 minute until fluffy. If the buttercream is too runny, add more powdered sugar as needed, 1 tablespoon (8 g) at a time, and if the frosting is too thick, add more milk. Transfer the buttercream to the prepared piping bag.

To assemble the macarons, pipe a ring of Honey Lavender Buttercream around the edges of each bottom shell. Then, spoon a bit of Lemon Lavender Curd in the center of each macaron, and top with another shell.

Let the macarons chill, covered, in the fridge overnight before serving, then let them sit at room temperature for 10 to 20 minutes before enjoying.

The Lemon Lavender Macarons will store well, covered, in the fridge for up to 5 days, or in the freezer, in an airtight container, for up to a month.

classic and timeless

Gathered in this chapter are macaron recipes that you may have seen before, perhaps in the form of cake when it comes to Black Forest Macarons (page 142), or in the form of cookies when it comes to Snickerdoodle Macarons (page 135)—which, by the way, is one of the best flavors I've ever tried! You will also find recipes that use simple, classic flavors and take them to the next level with beautiful decorations, such as the Raspberry Macarons (page 138), Nutella Macarons (page 141) and Pistachio Macarons (page 132). And have fun baking colorful and beautiful Birthday Cake Macarons (page 131) and Cotton Candy Macarons (page 147). They will be an absolute sensation with anyone who tries them!

birthday cake macarons

Birthday Cake Macarons are worthy of a celebration! These colorful macarons are a traditional flavor with which you can't go wrong. That being said, they're also far from plain! The soft, gooey, sprinkle-filled Edible Birthday Cake Batter filling takes the texture to another dimension, and the Cream Cheese Frosting adds a tanginess to the sweet ensemble.

yield: 20 (1½" [4-cm]) macaron sandwiches

1 batch Plain Macaron Shells (page 24) dyed with a few drops of blue gel food coloring. Sprinkle 3 tbsp (28 g) of pink nonpareil sprinkles on top of the shells before baking.

cream cheese frosting

6 tbsp (85 g) cream cheese, softened

3 tbsp (42 g) unsalted butter, softened

1 cup (125 g) powdered sugar, sifted, plus more as needed

½ tbsp (7 ml) milk or water, as needed

½ tsp cake batter flavoring (or ½ tsp vanilla and ⅛ tsp almond extract)

edible birthday cake batter

2 tbsp (28 g) unsalted butter, softened

2 tbsp (25 g) granulated sugar

¼ cup (32 g) almond flour or heat-treated all-purpose flour (see Note), plus more as needed

½ tbsp (7 ml) milk, plus more as needed

½ tsp cake batter extract (or ½ tsp vanilla and ⅛ tsp almond extract)

1 tbsp (14 g) nonpareils sprinkles

tools

Piping bag

Open star piping tip (¼" [6 mm] in diameter) or piping tip of your choice

First, make the Plain Macaron Shells, following the directions on page 24 and adding a few drops of blue gel food coloring when instructed. Right after popping the air bubbles out, sprinkle some pink nonpareil sprinkles on top of the shells before baking.

Line a piping bag with a piping tip to pipe the Cream Cheese Frosting onto the shells. Set aside. To make the Cream Cheese Frosting, beat the cream cheese and butter in a large bowl with a mixer at medium-high speed for 2 minutes, until light and fluffy. With the mixer off, add the powdered sugar to the bowl, and mix on low speed until combined. Once you no longer see streaks of dry powdered sugar, beat the mixture on medium-high speed for 1 minute. If the frosting is too runny, add more powdered sugar, 1 tablespoon (8 g) at a time, and if the frosting is too thick, add milk or water, 1 teaspoon at a time. Add the cake batter flavoring and mix to combine. Transfer the frosting to the prepared piping bag.

To make the Edible Birthday Cake Batter, beat the butter in a large bowl with a mixer for 30 seconds. Since it's a small amount of butter, it's best to use a hand mixer. Add the sugar, and beat the mixture for another 30 seconds. Add the flour, milk and cake batter flavoring to the bowl, and beat just until incorporated. The mixture should be thick and smooth like a cookie dough. If the dough is too soft and sticky, add 1 teaspoon of flour at a time to thicken. If the dough is too dry, add a few drops of milk or water.

To assemble the macarons, pipe dots of Cream Cheese Frosting around the edges of each bottom shell. Spoon some of the Edible Birthday Cake Batter in the center of each macaron, and top with another shell. Let the macarons chill, covered, in the fridge overnight before serving, then let them sit at room temperature for 10 to 20 minutes before enjoying. The Birthday Cake Macarons will store well, covered, in the fridge for up to 5 days, or in the freezer, in an airtight container, for up to a month.

note: If using all-purpose flour for the Edible Birthday Cake Batter, you will need to heat treat it. Microwave the flour in a heat-proof bowl for 1 minute, stirring halfway through. Let it cool down completely before using.

pistachio macarons

Pistachio Macarons are a classic, an all-time favorite, and it's easy to understand why. Pistachios naturally taste lightly sweet and buttery with a smooth finish. In this variation, a delicious Pistachio Ganache fills the Pistachio Macaron Shells. The ganache is velvety and brimming with nutty pistachio flavor—and so are the shells, which are made out of pistachios and topped with even more pistachios. If I had to pick just one flavor to make out of the whole book, this would definitely be it.

yield: 20 (1½" [4-cm]) macaron sandwiches

1 batch Pistachio Macaron Shells (page 38) dyed with a few drops of green gel food coloring

pistachio ganache
1½ cups (255 g) chopped white chocolate
½ cup (120 ml) heavy cream
3 tbsp (45 g) pistachio paste
1 tsp invert sugar (see Note)

for decoration
⅓ cup (56 g) chopped white chocolate
¼ cup (24 g) ground pistachios

tools
Piping bag
Round piping tip (½" [1.3 cm] in diameter) or piping tip of your choice

First, make the Pistachio Macaron Shells, following the directions on page 38 and adding a few drops of green gel food coloring when instructed.

Line a piping bag with a piping tip to pipe the Pistachio Ganache onto the shells. Set it aside.

To make the Pistachio Ganache, place the chocolate in a medium heat-proof bowl. Set it aside.

In a small pan, bring the cream, pistachio paste and invert sugar to a boil over medium heat, stirring occasionally to incorporate the ingredients and break up the pistachio paste. As soon as the mixture begins to bubble, turn off the heat.

Pour the hot cream over the chocolate through a fine-mesh sieve to catch any bits of pistachios. Using the back of a spatula, press the solids in the sieve to release any liquid. Cover the bowl with a towel and let it sit for 1 minute.

Then, use a whisk to gently incorporate the chocolate and cream mixture. Continue to whisk gently until the chocolate has completely melted. If you notice lumps of chocolate in the ganache, you can strain them out, or heat the bowl in the microwave for 5-second intervals, stirring in between to ensure all the bits of chocolate have melted. However, be careful to avoid overheating the chocolate so it doesn't become lumpy and thick.

To make the ganache extra smooth and glossy, transfer it to a narrow measuring cup and use an immersion blender to emulsify the ganache for 30 to 45 seconds. This is an optional step. The reason why a narrow measuring cup is necessary is so the blades of the blender won't be exposed while emulsifying, which would incorporate unnecessary air into the ganache.

(continued)

Place a piece of plastic wrap directly on top of the ganache so a skin doesn't form, and then set the ganache aside until it cools to room temperature. It will thicken as it cools down. After about 2 hours, the ganache should be ready to be piped. If it is still too soft, place it in the fridge for 10 to 20 minutes, then give it a good stir before transferring it to the prepared piping bag.

To decorate the top shells, place the chocolate in a heat-proof bowl and microwave it for 15-second intervals, stirring in between, until completely melted. Dip the top of 20 shells in the melted chocolate, and place them on a baking sheet. While the chocolate is still wet, top the shells with ground pistachios.

To assemble the macarons, pipe the Pistachio Ganache on each bottom shell. Top with a decorated shell.

Let the macarons chill, covered, in the fridge overnight before serving, then let them sit at room temperature for 10 to 20 minutes before enjoying.

The Pistachio Macarons will store well, covered, in the fridge for up to 5 days, or in the freezer, in an airtight container, for up to a month.

note: Invert sugar makes the ganache silky, stable and shiny, but is not necessary otherwise.

If you can't find invert sugar or don't want to follow an online recipe to make your own, simply leave it out.

snickerdoodle macarons

When you bite into a Snickerdoodle Macaron, first you'll notice the crunchy outside shell, thanks to the cinnamon sugar that gets sprinkled on top before baking. Next, you'll be amazed by the inside of the shell, which is chewy and soft, followed by the incredible fillings: a tangy Cinnamon Cream Cheese Frosting surrounding an edible Snickerdoodle Cookie Dough. The texture of the first bite is a whole experience on its own, and the taste is unbelievable. I didn't tell my husband what the flavor was and had him guess when he tried it. He immediately nailed it: Snickerdoodle, he guessed. Indeed, one of the best flavors I've ever accomplished!

yield: 20 (1½" [4-cm]) macaron sandwiches

1 batch Plain Macaron Shells (page 24). Sprinkle the shells with the Cinnamon Sugar Mix before baking.

cinnamon sugar mix

1 tbsp (12 g) granulated sugar
2 tsp (5 g) cinnamon

cinnamon cream cheese frosting

6 tbsp (85 g) cream cheese, softened
3 tbsp (42 g) unsalted butter, softened
1 cup (125 g) powdered sugar, sifted, plus more as needed
1 tsp cinnamon, plus more to taste
½ tbsp (7 ml) milk or water, as needed
¼ tsp vanilla extract

snickerdoodle cookie dough

2 tbsp (28 g) unsalted butter, softened
2 tbsp (25 g) granulated sugar
¼ cup (32 g) almond flour or heat-treated all-purpose flour (see Note), plus more as needed
½ tbsp (7 ml) milk
¼ tsp vanilla extract
¼ tsp cinnamon

tools

Piping bag
Round piping tip (¼" [6 mm] in diameter) or piping tip of your choice

First, prepare the Cinnamon Sugar Mix by combining the sugar and cinnamon in a small bowl. Then, make the Plain Macaron Shells, following the directions on page 24. Right after piping the shells, tapping the trays and poking the air bubbles out, sprinkle the Cinnamon Sugar Mix on top of the shells before baking. Be careful not to weigh down the macarons with too much of the mixture.

Line a piping bag with a piping tip to pipe the Cinnamon Cream Cheese Frosting onto the shells. Set aside.

(continued)

To make the Cinnamon Cream Cheese Frosting, beat the cream cheese and butter in a large bowl with a mixer at medium-high speed for 2 minutes, until light and fluffy. With the mixer off, add the powdered sugar and cinnamon to the bowl, and mix on low speed until combined. Once you no longer see streaks of dry powdered sugar, beat the mixture on medium-high speed for 1 minute. Add the vanilla and mix to combine. If the frosting is too runny, add more powdered sugar as needed, 1 tablespoon (8 g) at a time, and if the frosting is too thick, add milk or water to thin it out, 1 teaspoon at a time, until the proper consistency is achieved. Add the vanilla and mix to combine. Transfer the frosting to the prepared piping bag.

To make the Snickerdoodle Cookie Dough, beat the butter in a large bowl with a mixer for 30 seconds. Since it's a very small amount of butter, it's best to use a hand mixer rather than a stand mixer. Add the sugar, and beat the mixture for another 30 seconds. Add the flour, milk, vanilla and cinnamon to the bowl, and beat just until incorporated. The mixture should be thick and smooth like a cookie dough. If the dough is too soft and sticky, add 1 teaspoon of flour at a time to make it thicker, and if the dough is too dry, add a few drops of milk or water to help it come together.

To assemble the macarons, pipe a ring of the Cinnamon Cream Cheese Frosting around the edges of each bottom shell. Spoon some of the Snickerdoodle Cookie Dough in the center of each macaron, and top with another shell.

Let the macarons chill, covered, in the fridge overnight before serving, then let them sit at room temperature for 10 to 20 minutes before enjoying.

The Snickerdoodle Macarons will store well, covered, in the fridge for up to 5 days, or in the freezer, in an airtight container, for up to a month.

note: If you are using all-purpose flour for the Snickerdoodle Cookie Dough, you will need to heat treat it. To do so, simply place the flour in a heat-proof bowl, and microwave it for 1 minute, stirring halfway through. Let it cool down completely before adding it to the batter.

raspberry macarons

These macarons are loaded with raspberry flavor! The shells are made with freeze-dried raspberry powder and filled with a delectable Raspberry Buttercream that's fluffy and sweet with the perfect sour kick. Using freeze-dried raspberry powder will give the frosting the most flavor because the process of freeze-drying removes the water content from the berry, which results in an intensely concentrated flavor.

yield: 20 (1½" [4-cm]) macaron sandwiches

1 batch Freeze-Dried Fruit Macaron Shells (page 36) using freeze-dried raspberry powder. Refer to the Painting the Bag Technique instructions on page 152 to color the batter with a few drops of fuchsia and pink gel food coloring.

raspberry buttercream

4 tbsp (56 g) unsalted butter, at room temperature

1½ cups (188 g) powdered sugar, sifted, plus more as needed

⅓ cup (30 g) freeze-dried raspberry powder

2 tbsp (30 ml) milk, as needed

tools

Piping bag

Round piping tip (½" [1.3 cm] in diameter) or piping tip of your choice

First, make the Freeze-Dried Fruit Macaron Shells, following the directions on page 36 and adding freeze-dried raspberry powder to the dry ingredients. Follow the instructions on page 152 of the Decorating Techniques chapter to dye the batter by painting the piping bag with a few drops of fuchsia and pink gel food coloring.

Line a piping bag with a piping tip to pipe the Raspberry Buttercream onto the shells. Set aside.

To make the Raspberry Buttercream, beat the butter in a large bowl with a mixer on medium-high speed for 2 minutes until fluffy. With the mixer off, add the powdered sugar and freeze-dried raspberry powder to the bowl, and mix on low speed until combined. Once you no longer see streaks of dry powdered sugar, beat the mixture on medium-high speed for 1 minute until smooth and creamy. If the buttercream is too runny, add more powdered sugar as needed, 1 tablespoon (8 g) at a time, and if the buttercream is too thick, add milk to thin it out, 1 teaspoon at a time, until the proper consistency is achieved. Transfer the buttercream to the prepared piping bag.

To assemble the macarons, pipe some of the Raspberry Buttercream on each bottom shell, then top with another shell.

Let the macarons chill, covered, in the fridge overnight before serving, then let them sit at room temperature for 10 to 20 minutes before enjoying.

The Raspberry Macarons will store well, covered, in the fridge for up to 5 days, or in the freezer, in an airtight container, for up to a month.

nutella macarons

Uncomplicated yet luxurious, these Nutella Macarons feature an easy-to-make, rich and remarkable Nutella Ganache sandwiched between Chocolate Macaron Shells. A touch of gold and drizzled chocolate on top allows for an understated yet elegant appearance that makes these macarons hard to forget.

yield: 20 (1¹/₂" [4-cm]) macaron sandwiches

1 batch Chocolate Macaron Shells (page 30)

nutella ganache
¹/₂ cup (85 g) chopped chocolate, or chocolate chips
¹/₄ cup (74 g) Nutella
3 tbsp (45 ml) heavy cream

for decoration
¹/₃ cup (56 g) chopped chocolate or chocolate chips
1 small sheet of edible gold leaf

tools
2 piping bags
Round piping tip (¹/₄" [6 mm] in diameter) or piping tip of your choice

First, make the Chocolate Macaron Shells, following the directions on page 30.

Line a piping bag with a piping tip to pipe the Nutella Ganache onto the shells. Set aside.

To make the Nutella Ganache, begin by placing the chocolate and the Nutella in a bowl. Set it aside.

In another heat-proof bowl, heat the cream in the microwave for 15-second intervals until it is very hot, but be careful that it doesn't boil over. Then, pour the hot cream over the chocolate and Nutella. Let it sit for 1 minute, then stir with a spatula until the chocolate has melted entirely. If you notice lumps of chocolate in the ganache, you can strain them out or heat the bowl in the microwave for 5-second intervals, stirring in between to ensure all the bits of chocolate have melted. However, be careful to avoid overheating the chocolate so it doesn't become lumpy and thick.

Set the ganache aside to cool to room temperature. You can place it in the fridge for about 30 minutes, or until thick, stirring every so often. If the ganache gets too hard, microwave it for 3- to 5-second intervals, stirring in between to obtain a smooth, spreadable consistency. When the ganache is at room temperature, thick and spreadable, transfer it to the prepared piping bag.

To decorate the top shells, place the chocolate in a heat-proof bowl and microwave it for 15-second intervals, stirring in between, until completely melted. Transfer the melted chocolate to a piping bag, use scissors to snip the end and drizzle chocolate over the top shells of the macarons. I did a swirl pattern on top of the shells. Once the chocolate has dried, tear small pieces of edible gold leaf and place them on top of the chocolate drizzle so they will stick.

To assemble the macarons, pipe some Nutella Ganache onto each bottom shell, then top with a decorated shell.

Let the macarons chill, covered, in the fridge overnight before serving, then let them sit at room temperature for 10 to 20 minutes before enjoying.

The Nutella Macarons will store well, covered, in the fridge for up to 5 days, or in the freezer, in an airtight container, for up to a month.

black forest macarons

Inspired by the classic Black Forest cake, these delicious macarons feature chocolate shells filled with a sweet and scrumptious Cherry Jam and a light Mascarpone Filling. Black Forest cake usually features whipped cream, but whipped cream isn't stable enough for a macaron filling. The Mascarpone Filling is an amazing alternative—just as fluffy as whipped cream, with a mildly sweet taste, which is a great complement to the syrupy cherry filling. And if you are feeling fancy, pipe some of the filling on top of the macarons and top them with a cherry, because, as we all know, everything is better with a cherry on top!

yield: 20 (1¹/₂" [4-cm]) macaron sandwiches

1 batch Chocolate Macaron Shells (page 30)

cherry jam
1 cup (150 g) chopped cherries
3 tbsp (36 g) granulated sugar
1 tbsp (15 ml) lemon juice
2 tsp (5 g) cornstarch
1 tbsp (15 ml) cold water

mascarpone filling (see note)
¹/₄ cup (60 ml) heavy whipping cream, cold
³/₄ cup (170 g) mascarpone cheese, cold
1–1¹/₂ cups (125–188 g) powdered sugar, sifted
¹/₄ tsp vanilla extract

for decoration
1 (1.5-oz [43-g]) chocolate bar
20 fresh cherries

tools
Piping bag
Round piping tip (¹/₄" [6 mm] in diameter) or piping tip of your choice
Vegetable peeler

First, make the Chocolate Macaron Shells, following the directions on page 30.

Line a piping bag with a piping tip to pipe the Mascarpone Filling onto the shells. Set aside.

Start by making the Cherry Jam. In a small saucepan, bring the cherries, sugar and lemon juice to a boil and let it simmer over medium heat for about 25 minutes, until the cherries are falling apart. Use the back of a spoon to help mash the cherries. If the mixture starts to dry out or stick to the pan, lower the heat and add a tablespoon (15 ml) of water to the pan.

In a small bowl, combine the cornstarch and cold water. Once the cherries are soft and have fallen apart, add the cornstarch mixture to the pan and bring it to a simmer, stirring constantly for 1 or 2 minutes until the jam is very thick.

Remove the pan from the heat and pour the jam into a bowl. Let it cool down, then cover it and place it in the fridge for about 2 hours until completely chilled.

(continued)

To make the Mascarpone Filling, be sure the cream is super cold and the mascarpone cheese isn't very liquid. Some brands of mascarpone cheese can be very runny, and you will need to drain it in a cheese cloth–lined strainer for a few hours in the fridge before using, or else the filling won't become stiff enough to pipe.

In a large bowl, whip the cream with an electric mixer at medium-high speed for 2 to 3 minutes, until stiff peaks form. Don't overwhip the cream, or it will separate and curdle. The peaks should be firm, but the cream shouldn't become chunky.

Once the cream is whipped, add the cold mascarpone cheese, 1 cup (125 g) of powdered sugar and the vanilla to the bowl. Mix on medium speed for another 1 to 2 minutes, until the ingredients are incorporated.

If the filling is too thin and soft, add the remaining powdered sugar and mix until incorporated. Transfer the filling to the prepared piping bag.

To assemble the macarons, pipe a ring of Mascarpone Filling around the edges of the bottom shells. Then, spoon some of the Cherry Jam in the middle of each macaron, and top with another shell.

To decorate the macarons, use a vegetable peeler to shave the chocolate bar. Roll the sides of the macarons in the chocolate shavings, or turn the macarons sideways and sprinkle the shavings around the edge of the macarons so they stick to the filling. Pipe a bit of Mascarpone Filling on top of the macarons, and place a cherry on top.

Let the macarons chill, covered in the fridge overnight before serving, then let them sit at room temperature for 10 to 20 minutes before enjoying.

The Black Forest Macarons will store well, covered, in the fridge for up to 5 days, or in the freezer, in an airtight container, for up to a month.

note: The Mascarpone Filling shouldn't be made in advance, as it has to be piped immediately after being made. It will hold up fine after it is piped, but it will start to deflate and won't pipe well if it sits in the bowl or in the piping bag.

romeo and juliet macarons

In Brazil we call the combination of guava and cheese "Romeo and Juliet." The flavor combination is a breakfast staple that is also used in pizza, pastries and empanadas. And of course, I had to turn it into a macaron flavor! These Romeo and Juliet Macarons are filled with a silky Cream Cheese Frosting which perfectly lightens up the sweet and robust guava jam. The best tip: Add a pinch of salt to the frosting to enhance the flavors and tie them together for an exquisite treat.

*See photo on page 129.

yield: 20 (1½" [4-cm]) macaron sandwiches

1 batch Plain Macaron Shells (page 24)

cream cheese frosting

6 tbsp (85 g) cream cheese, softened
3 tbsp (42 g) unsalted butter, softened
1 cup (125 g) powdered sugar, sifted, plus more as needed
½ tbsp (7 ml) milk or water, as needed
¼ tsp vanilla extract
¼ tsp salt

for the filling

¼ cup (84 g) guava jam (see Note)

for decoration

⅓ cup (56 g) chopped white chocolate
3 tbsp (28 g) heart and white sprinkles

tools

Piping bag
Round piping tip (¼" [6 mm] in diameter) or piping tip of your choice

First, make the Plain Macaron Shells, following the directions on page 24.

Line a piping bag with a piping tip to pipe the Cream Cheese Frosting onto the shells. Set aside.

To make the Cream Cheese Frosting, beat the cream cheese and butter in a large bowl with a mixer at medium-high speed for 2 minutes, until light and fluffy. With the mixer off, add the powdered sugar to the bowl, and mix on low speed until combined. Once you no longer see streaks of dry powdered sugar, beat the mixture on medium-high speed for 1 minute. If the frosting is too runny, add more powdered sugar as needed, 1 tablespoon (8 g) at a time, and if the frosting is too thick, add milk or water to thin it out, 1 teaspoon at a time, until the proper consistency is achieved. Add the vanilla and salt, then mix to combine. Transfer the frosting to the prepared piping bag.

To decorate the top shells, place the chocolate in a small heat-proof bowl and microwave it for 15-second intervals, stirring in between, until completely melted. Dip the top half of 20 shells in the melted chocolate, and place them on a baking sheet lined with parchment or silicone, for easy removal later. While the chocolate is still wet, sprinkle some hearts and white sprinkles on top of the shells.

To assemble the macarons, pipe a ring of the Cream Cheese Frosting around the edges of each bottom shell. Then, spoon some of the guava jam in the center of each macaron, and top with a decorated shell.

Let the macarons chill, covered, in the fridge overnight before serving, then let them sit at room temperature for 10 to 20 minutes before enjoying.

The Romeo and Juliet Macarons will store well, covered, in the fridge for up to 5 days, or in the freezer, in an airtight container, for up to a month.

note: You can get guava jam online and at many grocery stores. Alternatively, you can also fill the macarons with guava paste by cutting a round, thin slice of paste and placing in the center of the macarons.

cotton candy macarons

These cheerful Cotton Candy Macarons capture all the fun of sweet childhood memories. The bright blue and pink shell colors and the fruity aroma of the Cotton Candy Buttercream filling add a nostalgic quality to these treats that will take you right back to carefree, sunshiny days filled with sugar-spun treats! Get ready to savor the irresistible sweetness of these whimsical Cotton Candy Macarons.

yield: 20 (1½" [4-cm]) macaron sandwiches

1 batch Plain Macaron Shells (page 24) made using the Multicolored Shells technique for two-tone shells demonstrated on page 148. Dye half the batter with pink gel food coloring, and dye the other half with sky blue gel food coloring.

cotton candy buttercream

6 tbsp (85 g) unsalted butter, at room temperature

1½ cups (188 g) powdered sugar, sifted, plus more as needed

2 tsp (10 ml) cotton candy syrup (see Note)

½ tbsp (7.5 ml) milk, as needed

tools

2 piping bags

Round piping tip (½" [1.3 cm] in diameter) or piping tip of your choice

First, make the Plain Macaron Shells, following the directions on page 24. Follow the instructions on page 148 of the Decorating Techniques chapter to make the two-toned shells. Dye half the batter with pink gel food coloring, and dye the other half with sky blue gel food coloring.

Line a piping bag with a piping tip to pipe the Cotton Candy Buttercream onto the shells. Set aside.

To make the Cotton Candy Buttercream, beat the butter in a large bowl with a mixer on medium-high speed for about 1 minute until it begins to get creamy. With the mixer off, add the powdered sugar and cotton candy syrup to the bowl, and mix on low speed until combined. Once you no longer see streaks of dry powdered sugar, whip the mixture on medium speed for 2 minutes. If the buttercream is too runny, add more powdered sugar as needed, 1 tablespoon (8 g) at a time, and if the buttercream is too thick, add milk to thin it out, 1 teaspoon at a time, until the proper consistency is achieved. Transfer the buttercream to the prepared piping bag.

To assemble the macarons, pipe the frosting on each bottom shell, and then top with another shell.

Let the macarons chill, covered in the fridge overnight before serving, then let them sit at room temperature for 10 to 20 minutes before enjoying.

The Cotton Candy Macarons will store well, covered, in the fridge for up to 5 days, or in the freezer, in an airtight container, for up to a month.

note: If you can't find any cotton candy syrup, you can use cotton candy flavoring. It can be found online pretty easily. If using cotton candy flavoring, add only ⅛ teaspoon to the buttercream after mixing the powdered sugar in, and then add more to taste if needed. Always proceed with caution, because these flavorings tend to be very concentrated and a little will go a long way.

decorating techniques

One of my favorite things to do when it comes to macarons is to think about the visual design. Decorating macarons can be done in many different ways! You can create a special design with two-toned shells, or you can add decorations to the shells after baking them. From sprinkles to melted chocolate, dried flowers to fruits, there are a lot of ways to elevate your designs and create macarons that look as good as they taste.

multicolored shells

There are two ways of making multicolored shells. The first way is to make different colors from one batch of macarons.

To do so, follow all the instructions to make the shells up until the macaronage stage. When you add the almond flour and powdered sugar to the meringue, stir just until the ingredients are combined and you see no more streaks of dry ingredients in the batter. At that point, stop stirring the batter.

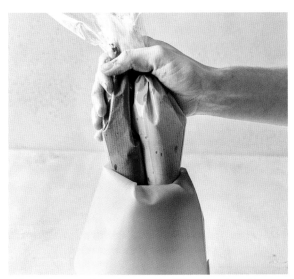

Place the two piping bags with different colored batter inside a larger piping bag.

Split the batter between bowls according to how many colors you are making. For example, if you are making two colors, split the batter between two different bowls. If making three colors, use three different bowls, and so forth. I don't recommend making more than five colors from just a single batch—otherwise, you won't have enough batter for each color.

Once the batter is divided, work with one bowl at a time, keeping the remaining bowls covered so the batter doesn't dry out.

Add the food coloring to the first bowl, then stir until the perfect consistency is achieved, as explained in the Plain Macaron Shells recipe (page 24). Transfer the batter to a piping bag with a sealed end, then secure the top of the bag with a tie and set it aside. Repeat this with each of the remaining bowls of batter you have set aside.

Pipe by applying even pressure around the bag so both colors come out at the same time.

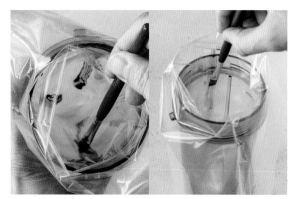

Brush the inside of the piping bags with food coloring.

Once you have all the colors you will use ready to go, use scissors to snip the ends of the bags, then place all the bags inside of a larger piping bag lined with a round piping tip (either ¼ or ½ inch [6 mm or 1.3 cm] wide). When placing the piping bags inside of the larger piping bag, try to keep the bags at the same level so the batters will all come out at the same time in equal amounts.

Then, you can pipe the batter normally, though you will notice the colored batters creating a swirl pattern in the shells.

If you want to make each shell a solid color, but make a few colors from the same batch, just follow the previous instructions above and transfer each colored batter to its own piping bag fitted with a round tip, ready to pipe. Pipe as many shells of each color as you'd like, or as your batter allows.

painting the bag technique

The "painting the bag" technique is a beautiful way to decorate your macarons. It gives a whimsical, gorgeous tie-dye effect to the shells.

This technique is very simple. Make the batter as you normally would according to the instructions on page 24, but before transferring it to a piping bag, dip a brush in gel food coloring, and lightly brush lines inside the piping bag.

Apply sprinkles to the shells right after piping them.

Make sure the lines start all the way at the bottom of the piping bag, where the piping tip is, or else it will take a while for the shells to start coming out with color in them. Then, transfer the batter to the piping bag and continue to follow the recipe as normal.

A valuable tip here is to not use too much color, or the macarons may crack once they bake due to the excess color and moisture.

sprinkles, spice and everything nice

You can add sprinkles and spices to your macaron shells before baking them. Sprinkle a small amount over the freshly piped shells while they are still wet.

Make sure the sprinkles aren't too heavy and aren't chocolate-based. Heavy sprinkles will sink in the batter and crack the shells, and chocolate-based sprinkles will melt.

When using spices, you can mix them with sugar, like I did with the Churros Macarons (page 79). The sugar gives the macarons a crackled top with a wonderful, slightly crunchy texture.

Dip the top of the macaron shell in melted white chocolate.

Dip half of the shell in melted white chocolate.

melted chocolate

This is definitely a technique I use a lot. I love drizzling melted chocolate over the macaron shells after baking them. This is even more fun if you top the drizzle with sprinkles or other powders.

The possibilities of toppings are endless: freeze-dried fruit powder, bee pollen, crushed nuts, sprinkles, gold leaf, mini marshmallows, dried flowers, chocolate chips, flaky salt, etc.

When drizzling melted chocolate over the macarons, I like to place the chocolate in a piping bag and snip the end with scissors to create a very small hole. You can drizzle the chocolate in a straight-line pattern by going back and forth with the piping bag, or you could do a swirl pattern by drawing several swirls over the shells.

Another way to decorate the shells with melted chocolate is to dip them in it. You could dip only the top shell in melted chocolate, or you could dip half of the whole macaron sandwich in it. I've even seen people completely coat their macarons in chocolate.

Apply sprinkles to the top of the wet chocolate to help it stick.

Besides chocolate, you could also use candy melts—they will dry, and you will be able to stack the macarons without them sticking, just as you would with chocolate.

You can also drizzle caramel or dulce de leche over the macarons. Just keep in mind that these toppings might stick and may not be the best alternative if you plan on stacking the macarons.

Airbrushing macaron shells.

Brush the top of shells with golden luster dust mixed with clear alcohol.

airbrushing

Airbrushing macaron shells is definitely an underrated technique. It gives the macarons a striking and impressive effect since the airbrushed colors are so vibrant and lively. To do this, you will need an airbrushing pen and some compatible food coloring. Airbrush the tops of the macarons after baking and let them dry before touching the macarons and filling them.

painting

A very popular technique is to paint the macaron shells. After the shells have baked and cooled, you can mix food coloring with a bit of clear liquor such as vodka to dilute it, then dip a food-safe brush in the mixture and paint on the tops. Be careful not to use too much liquid, as it will dissolve the macaron shell. Instead of food coloring, you can also mix the clear liquor with a powder such as edible luster dust. Mix until a thin paste is formed, then dip a brush in and paint on the shells.

If you don't want to use clear liquor to do this, you can use water, but be aware that the water won't evaporate as fast as the alcohol does, so it might make the shells soggy or cause them to disintegrate.

Here are some other decoration ideas:

- Pipe frosting on top of the macarons, then top them with cherries, nuts, berries or popcorn.

- Brûlée the top of the shells by brushing the shells with a very tiny amount of water, then sprinkling granulated sugar on top. Use a blow torch to toast the sugar, then let it cool down before enjoying.

- Coat the sides of the macarons where the frosting is with sprinkles, shredded coconut, shaved chocolate, etc.

- Use a fun piping tip to pipe the filling—a simple design technique that makes a statement!

- Sprinkle edible luster dust over the shells after baking for a shimmery look.

troubleshooting

We have arrived at the gold mine of all macaron learning: the troubleshooting tips!

Mastering macarons is like becoming a problem-solving detective. Whenever an issue arises, you have to dig deep and try to find out what caused it in order to avoid it next time.

In this guide, you will find some information that may seem contradictory—for instance, hollow macarons are caused by overmixing or undermixing the batter. While that may seem like a contradiction, it simply means that you have to find the sweet spot, the perfect balance, when it comes to making macarons.

Also keep in mind that some issues, like high oven temperature, for example, can cause more than one outcome. Since there are so many variables when it comes to making macarons, anytime something goes wrong, the result might vary depending on all the other factors.

bumpy macaron shells

Bumpy macaron shells can have air pockets on the surface or a shaggy look and texture. This issue can happen because:

- You undermixed the batter. how to fix it: Mix until the batter flows off a spatula slowly and effortlessly, and the batter that falls back into the bowl incorporates with the remaining batter within 10 to 15 seconds.

- You used lumpy almond flour. how to fix it: Use a fine-mesh sieve to sift the almond flour, or look for a brand that is already finely sifted.

- You didn't pop the air bubbles. how to fix it: Use a toothpick or a scribe to pop any bubbles that form on the surface of the shells after piping the batter.

browned or faded macaron shells

Browned or faded macaron shells happen especially with lighter colors because, as they bake, they fade and lose their vibrancy or become brown. This issue can happen because:

- You overbaked your shells. how to fix it: Bake until you can move a macaron and it doesn't feel jiggly. If you gently touch the top of a shell, it shouldn't feel soft. Remove the macarons from the oven as soon as that happens.

- Your oven temperature was too high. how to fix it: Use an oven thermometer to ensure you are using the proper temperature, or experiment with lower temperatures to see what suits your oven best.

- Another tip is to cover the macarons with foil during the last 5 minutes of baking. To keep the colors from fading, you can also add more food coloring to your batter, but be careful, as this may cause flat, crispy macaron shells (see page 156).

concave macaron shells

Concave macaron shells are those without a bottom skin, where the bottom of the macaron is curved in. This issue can happen because:

- Your oven temperature was too low. how to fix it: Use an oven thermometer to ensure you are using the proper temperature, or experiment with higher oven temperatures to see what suits your oven best.

- Your macarons were baking too far from the heat source. how to fix it: Move the oven racks around to find the optimal spot to bake the macarons for your specific oven.

- You underbaked your shells. how to fix it: Bake until you can move a macaron and it doesn't feel jiggly. If you gently touch the top of a shell, it shouldn't feel soft.

- You used a greasy baking surface. how to fix it: If your silicone mats are greasy, soak them in warm, soapy water mixed with vinegar, or considering buying a new mat. And always wipe down your mats with vinegar before starting.

cracked macaron shells

Cracked macaron shells or "volcano macarons" are shells that crack instead of becoming smooth and round. They often also lack feet. This issue can happen because:

- Your oven temperature was too high. how to fix it: Use an oven thermometer to ensure you are using the proper temperature, or experiment with lower temperatures to see what suits your oven best.

- The heat in your oven is uneven. how to fix it: Place a few oven thermometers inside the oven in different places to identify any hot spots to avoid. For example, my oven is hot in the left front side, so I know to rotate my trays after the first 5 minutes of baking and position them slightly to the right while baking.

- You didn't rest your macarons enough. how to fix it: Rest the macarons until they feel dry to the touch, or try a no-rest technique.

- You used a baking tray with a tall rim. how to fix it: Experiment with rimless baking sheets for optimal airflow.

(continued)

- You used dark baking sheets. how to fix it: Try using silver aluminum sheets instead of dark steel ones.

- You underwhipped the meringue. how to fix it: Be sure to whip the meringue until stiff peaks are formed (see page 11).

flat, crispy macaron shells

Flat, crispy, deflated macaron shells can happen because:

- You overmixed the batter. how to fix it: Mix the batter until it flows off a spatula slowly and effortlessly and has a thick honey consistency. If the batter is flowing continuously and too fast, it's overmixed.

- You used too much food coloring. how to fix it: Go easy on the food coloring, especially if you are a beginner, until you are able to comfortably add a lot of color to the shells.

- Your oven temperature was too high. how to fix it: Use an oven thermometer to ensure you are using the proper temperature, or experiment with lower temperatures to see what suits your oven best.

hollow macaron shells

Hollow macarons are a hot topic in the macaron community. A lot of people seem to worry that achieving full macarons right out of the oven is an absolute must. I get so many messages from people who are disheartened or have lost their motivation to bake because they can't seem to "get rid of" hollow macarons. But I am here to put you at ease. Most of the time, the shells fill up after maturing in the fridge, so don't be worried if your shells seem a bit hollow immediately after baking. Your shells should have a solid structure, formed feet and a sturdy top, and as long as these qualities are present, the macarons should fill up as they mature. If your shells have a large gap in the middle and the top is fragile and crumbling easily to the touch, that's when you have a problem that needs fixing. Take a look at the following suggestions, try making one alteration at a time, write down your results and continue to perfect the little details.

Hollow macaron shells can happen because:

- You overmixed or undermixed the batter. how to fix it: Mix until the batter flows off a spatula slowly and effortlessly, and the batter that falls back into the bowl incorporates with the remaining batter within 10 to 15 seconds.

- Your meringue was broken from being either over- or underwhipped. how to fix it: Whip the meringue at a lower speed, until it achieves stiff peaks. Underwhipped meringue can become weak and break, and overwhipped meringue will make the protein bonds so tight that they will squeeze out the air and water particles. Refer to page 11 for a description of the perfect meringue consistency.

- Your oven temperature was too high or too low. how to fix it: Use an oven thermometer to ensure you are using the proper temperature, or experiment with lower temperatures to see what suits your oven best.

- You underbaked your shells. how to fix it: Bake until you can move a macaron and it doesn't feel jiggly. If you gently touch the top of a shell, it shouldn't feel soft.

more tips to avoid hollows and gaps in your macarons:

- Use egg white powder in the shells. This has helped so many bakers to get fuller shells, because the egg white powder strengthens the meringue.

- Whip the meringue low and slow. Use a low speed, and whip it for a long time, as this will prevent overwhipping.

Lopsided Macaron Shells

Lopsided macarons will usually have very small feet or no feet at all on one side, and have taller feet on the other side. This issue can happen because:

- You rested your macarons too long. how to fix it: Rest the macarons until they feel dry to the touch, or try a no-rest technique. If the macarons rest too much, some of the structures of the meringue may begin to break down, especially if the weather is humid.

- You used a baking tray with a tall rim. how to fix it: Experiment with rimless baking sheets for optimal airflow.

- The heat in your oven is uneven. how to fix it: Place a few oven thermometers inside the oven in different places to identify any hot spots to avoid. For example, my oven is hot in the left front side, so I know to rotate my trays after the first 5 minutes of baking and position them slightly to the right while baking.

macaron shells with no feet

Macaron shells with no feet or very tiny feet can happen because:

- Your oven temperature was too low. how to fix it: Use an oven thermometer to ensure you are using the proper temperature, or experiment with higher oven temperatures to see what suits your oven best.

- You rested your macarons too long. how to fix it: Rest the macarons until they feel dry to the touch, or try a no-rest technique. If the macarons rest too much, some of the protein structures of the meringue may begin to break down, especially if the weather is humid.

- Your macarons were baking too far from the heat source. how to fix it: Move the oven racks around to find the optimal spot to bake the macarons for your specific oven.

misshapen macaron shells

Misshapen macaron shells aren't perfectly round; they are spread out, without a defined circle shape. This can happen because:

- You overmixed the batter. how to fix it: Mix the batter until it flows off a spatula slowly and effortlessly and has a thick honey consistency. If the batter is flowing continuously and too fast, it's overmixed.

- Your piping technique lacks control. how to fix it: Pipe steadily for a few seconds, applying gentle pressure to release the batter, then lift the piping bag and twist it at the top with a swirl motion to stop dispensing batter. Using bag ties to secure the ends of the piping bags closed will give you a chance to control the bags better since you'll be able to hold them in the middle.

- You piped your macarons onto parchment paper. how to fix it: Parchment paper causes wrinkly bottoms that can make macarons look misshapen. Try using silicone mats or Teflon mats instead of parchment paper.

- You banged the trays too much. how to fix it: Don't bang the trays too much or too hard—just enough to release a few air bubbles.

porous macaron shells

Porous macaron shells present a surface full of tiny holes, and they often lack feet. This issue can happen because:

- Your meringue was broken from being either over- or underwhipped. how to fix it: Whip the meringue at a lower speed, until it achieves stiff peaks. Underwhipped meringue can become weak and break, and overwhipped meringue will make the protein bonds so tight that they will squeeze out the air and water particles. Refer to page 11 for a description of the perfect meringue consistency.

- Grease or water particles got into the meringue. how to fix it: Wipe down all tools and materials with vinegar before making macarons. Make sure no yolk bits or water particles get in the meringue.

- Your almond flour was oily. how to fix it: Switch almond flour brands, get a fresh bag or dry the almond flour in the oven as indicated in Chapter 1 (page 14).

- You used too much cocoa powder. how to fix it: Reduce the amount of cocoa powder added. Try to aim for about 5 grams per 100 grams of egg whites.

- You used cocoa powder with a high fat content. how to fix it: Look for a brand with a low fat content. The brand I use has 0.5 grams of fat per tablespoon.

ruffled feet

Ruffled feet are super tall and spread outward past the diameter of the top of the shell. This issue can happen because:

- You overwhipped the meringue. how to fix it: Whip the meringue at a lower speed, until it achieves stiff peaks. Overwhipped meringue will make the protein bonds so tight that they will squeeze out the air and water particles. Refer to page 11 for a description of the perfect meringue consistency.

- You overmixed the batter. how to fix it: Mix the batter until it flows off a spatula slowly and effortlessly and has a thick honey consistency. If the batter is flowing continuously and too fast, it's overmixed.

- Your oven temperature was too high. how to fix it: Use an oven thermometer to ensure you are using the proper temperature, or experiment with lower temperatures to see what suits your oven best.

soft, fragile macaron shells

Soft shells are super fragile and can break easily when touched. They are often hollow with a paper-thin layer on top. This issue can happen because:

- Your meringue was broken from being either over- or underwhipped. how to fix it: Whip the meringue at a lower speed, until it achieves stiff peaks. Underwhipped meringue can become weak and break, and overwhipped meringue will make the protein bonds so tight that they will squeeze out the air and water particles. Refer to page 11 for a description of the perfect meringue consistency.

- You overmixed the batter. how to fix it: Mix the batter until it flows off a spatula slowly and effortlessly and has a thick honey consistency. If the batter is flowing continuously and too fast, it's overmixed.

- You underbaked your shells. how to fix it: Bake until you can move a macaron and it doesn't feel jiggly. If you gently touch the top of a shell, it shouldn't feel soft.

speckled macaron shells

Speckled macaron shells have blotchy tops. This issue can happen because:

- Your almond flour was oily. how to fix it: Switch almond flour brands, get a fresh bag or dry the almond flour in the oven as indicated in Chapter 1 (page 14).

- You used too much cocoa powder. how to fix it: Reduce the amount of cocoa powder added. Try to aim for 5 grams per 100 grams of egg whites.

- You used cocoa powder with a high fat content. how to fix it: Look for a brand with a low fat content. The brand I use has 0.5 grams of fat per tablespoon.

- You pulsed the dry ingredients in a food processor. how to fix it: Look for a finely sifted brand of almond flour so you don't have to pulse the dry ingredients in the food processor, which can cause the almond flour to release oils.

- You overmixed the batter. how to fix it: Mix the batter until it flows off a spatula slowly and effortlessly and has a thick honey consistency. If the batter is flowing continuously and too fast, it's overmixed.

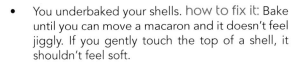

- You underbaked your shells. how to fix it: Bake until you can move a macaron and it doesn't feel jiggly. If you gently touch the top of a shell, it shouldn't feel soft.

sticky macaron shells

Sticky macaron shells stick to the mat after they've been baked. Sometimes the whole bottom of the shells will stick, or they'll just stick in a few spots. This issue can happen because:

- You underbaked your shells. how to fix it: Bake until you can move a macaron and it doesn't feel jiggly. If you gently touch the top of a shell, it shouldn't feel soft.

- Your oven temperature was too low. how to fix it: Use an oven thermometer to ensure you are using the proper temperature, or experiment with higher oven temperatures to see what suits your oven best.

- You didn't let the macarons cool down before peeling them off the mat. how to fix it: Make sure the macarons have cooled down completely before removing them from the baking mat.

wrinkled macaron shells

Wrinkled macaron shells will have a rugged surface. This issue can happen because:

- Your almond flour was oily. how to fix it: Switch almond flour brands, get a fresh bag or dry the almond flour as indicated in Chapter 1 (page 14).

- You used too much cocoa powder. how to fix it: Reduce the amount of cocoa powder. Try to aim for 5 grams per 100 grams of egg whites.

- You used cocoa powder with a high fat content. how to fix it: Look for a brand with a low fat content, about 0.5 grams of fat per tablespoon.

- You overmixed the batter. how to fix it: Mix the batter until it flows off a spatula slowly and effortlessly and has a thick honey consistency. If the batter is flowing too fast, it's overmixed.

- You overwhipped the meringue. how to fix it: Whip the meringue at a lower speed, until it achieves stiff peaks. Refer to page 11 for a description of the perfect meringue consistency.

- You overheated the sugar and egg white syrup. how to fix it: Heat the syrup over a double boiler just until the sugar melts, and immediately remove it from the heat after that.

acknowledgments

I'd like to acknowledge the wonderful macaron community first and foremost. This book wouldn't be here if it wasn't for each and every one of you. Thank you for your support and for cheering me on, for trusting me to be your teacher and also for teaching me so much. Thank you to my followers and readers for all the love.

To my son, Luke, you are such a light in my life. I appreciate every single moment with you. You truly are the sweetest boy in the whole world, and I am thankful for your presence, joy and kindness. You make my life so rich and fulfilled!

To my husband, Brian, you are the best partner I could have ever asked for. Your unconditional support means the world to me. Thank you for encouraging me to do what I love, and for being such a good human and someone to look up to.

To my dad, Celso, and my mom, Regina, Mãe e Pai! Thank you for showing so much support and love for me and what I do! Thank you for always believing in me. You've given me every tool necessary for me to be who I am today, and for that I am grateful. Even though you are thousands of miles away, we are closer than ever!

To my sisters, Marina and Aline, you two are the reason why I do what I do. You are my best friends. I am so lucky and grateful to be your sister. Thank you for being there for me and cheering me on. I am so proud of you two! You inspire me so much!

To my grandparents, Neco, Mabilia and Amalia, for being the base of everything and instilling in me the love for cooking and baking, hard work and resilience.

To my aunt Rosy, for being a role model and friend to me!

To everyone at Page Street Publishing, especially Emily Taylor, my sweet editor, for being kind and brilliant. To Meg Baskis and the whole team! And to Laura Benton, the designer of my book and cover. Thank you all so much for believing in me!

about the author

Camila Hurst is a self-taught baker who was born and raised in Brazil and moved to the United States in 2011. In 2017 she started her blog, Pies and Tacos, which quickly grew and became a household name for macaron learning. Camila is a food photographer, recipe developer and author. Her first cookbook, *Fantastic Filled Cupcakes*, was published in 2019. *Macaron School* is her second cookbook. Her work has been featured on BuzzFeed, Tasty, The Bake Feed, The Food Network and feedfeed, among others. Camila currently lives in Florida with her husband and son.

index